BLACK WIDOW

De-webbing The Journey of Grief

Faye J. Williams

The Black Widow Copyright © 2016 by Faye J. Williams. All rights reserved. This book or any portion thereof may not be reproduced or used in any manner whatsoever without the express written permission of the publisher except for the use of brief quotations in a book review.

I have tried to recreate events, locales and conversations from my memories of them. Some names and identifying details have been changed to protect the privacy of individuals. I may have changed some identifying characteristics and details such as physical properties, occupations and places of residence.

Although the author and publisher have made every effort to ensure that the information in this book was correct at press time, the author and publisher do not assume and hereby disclaim any liability to any party for any loss, damage, or disruption caused by errors or omissions, whether such errors or omissions result from negligence, accident, or any other cause. Views expressed in this publication do not necessarily reflect the views of the publisher.

Cover Illustration Kingdom Grahpica
Editing by Jessica Williams

Printed in the United States of America
First Printing, 2016
ISBN:-13:9781941749616
Library of Congress Catalog Number

4-P Publishing
Chattanooga, TN 37411

Acknowledgments

First of all, to God be the Glory. For without Him I would not be able to think a thought, let alone write a sentence.

This book, The Black Widow, is dedicated to the loving memory of my late husband, John Wesley Williams, Sr.

As my words became sentences, and my sentences became paragraphs and my paragraphs became chapters and my chapters became my book there are many people who helped me and encouraged me along the way. To my BETA readers; Valoria V. Armstrong, Irene B. Chapman, Jewell B. Cousin, Judith S. Kilgore and Anne J. McGhee, I extend a hardy thank you for your invaluable and constructive suggestions, corrections and criticisms as I navigated this difficult endeavor.

To my children; Ashley, Donna, Jade, John, Lisa and Veronica, I thank you for your constant love and support. Especially during your father's sickness and death. Sometimes 'thank you' seems inadequate but I know not a better way to express my gratitude. We are family!

To Jayveun, my grandson, who was only 9 years old at the time, exemplified such maturity and courage. During those short nine years J.W. taught Jayveun many lessons about life, love, manhood and God. Lessons that will continue to be with Jayveun throughout his life. There was a special bond between grandfather and grandson.

Many thanks to Myra, Mary, Kellye, Sarah, Rosetta, Connie, Tim, Michael, Jean and countless others for your words of encouragement as I pushed forward to bring this book alive and complete.

To my publisher, 4-P Publishing, my editor, Jessica Williams and my book cover designer, Eric Finley, who totally developed exactly what I wanted, thank you.

To my late mother, Mrs. Louise Kilgore Jones, who never saw the book as a finished product often urged me on. As a widow herself, Mama understood the difficulties that I endured as I struggled, often through tears, to complete this project. Mama died a few short months before this book was published.

Mama and J.W. were two of my biggest cheerleaders!

Contents

ACKNOWLEDGMENTS 3

INTRODUCTION 11

REMEMBER DECEMBER............................... 13

THE FOG CLEARED 25

ROOM 257.. 33

WHEN SOMETHING IS WRONG WITH MY BABY...SOMETHING IS WRONG WITH ME 39

STARTING ALL OVER AGAIN 51

HOME SWEET HOME...OR NOT 55

J. W., PLEASE WORK WITH ME 63

THE FALL OF A TOWER................................ 69

THE GRADUATION 75

THANK YOU, LORD.. 79

GOOD BYE MY SWEET LOVE, GOOD BYE MY FRIEND 95

'HOLD ON, GOD WILL SEE YOU THROUGH' 101

2 TIMOTHY 4:7 111

NOW WHAT? 115

UNDERSTANDING AND ACCEPTANCE ..121

THE ANATOMY OF GRIEF 125

PAUSE BEFORE YOU POST 129

THE STRENGTH OF OTHERS 135

EMBRACING A NEW NORMAL 143

A NEW SEASON 151

HEALING NOT HEALED 155

IT'S TIME TO FLY 161

KNOW YOUR WORTH 165

EPILOGUE 171

Introduction

I wrote this book not as a vehicle to drive you through the process of grieving but as a tool to help you on your journey. Countless women become widows on a daily basis. Sometimes a husband's death will occur after a prolonged illness and other times the death is sudden and without warning. However, it happens, the widow is left with the grappling responsibility of figuring out life going forward.

This book chronicles my path, my 'de-webbing' to a place less painful than where I

The Black Widow

began, it's called 'healing'. I am a work in progress.

When I made the decision to write this book, I had no idea that it would be so difficult. Healing is a process and where I've started to heal, writing this book has torn open my wounds anew.

The Black Widow is not to suggest that a black widow suffers more than any other widow, rather it is my ethnicity and my status.

I am Faye J. Williams and this is my story.

CHAPTER 1

Remember December

It's funny how things can start and stop around the same time. I met my husband, John Wesley Williams, Sr., in May of 1983 and I was forced to say good-bye to him in May of 2014.

My husband died on a Tuesday morning. Not just any Tuesday morning. It was a bright, sunny Tuesday morning. May 27th, the day after Memorial Day to be exact.

Historically, J.W. who had always been healthy, started experiencing health issues that were beginning to mount and in some instances become more aggressive.

The Black Widow

As with everything, there has to be a starting point and for J.W. that date is December 9, 2011. It was a cold night but it was December so no surprise there. Since before we married, J.W. burned wood to keep down the fuel cost plus he enjoyed making fires which warmed the house nicely and emitted a nice aroma. On this particular night, I had gone to bed a little early and he said that he'd be up shortly.

Although I chose to start my story as of December 9, 2011, there had been health concerns prior to this date. A few of his conditions included severe chronic obstructive pulmonary disease (COPD), Sleep Apnea, Parkinson's disease and Diabetes. As a result he used oxygen all the time except when we went to church. He didn't want to fool with the portable cylinders but he always had an inhaler. Also he didn't use his oxygen when he fed the wood burner, but he was always careful to make his actions as quickly and deliberately as possible. However, because of his weakened condition, I often helped with the fire. This night was different. I was tired and I had an early magnetic resonance imaging (MRI) appointment the next morning. So when I went to bed I fell fast asleep. Normally I awake during the night but on this night I slept the night through. The next morning, around 5:00a.m., I noticed that my husband wasn't next to me in bed and I could hear the television in the kitchen blaring. I tried to rest for at least another thirty minutes before it was time for me to rise and shine. I tossed and turned a few minutes and finally decided to get up because the TV was driving me nuts. So I snatched the covers aside and angrily headed to the kitchen to blast him for having the television so loud. When I reached the kitchen there was no J.W. Then I noticed that the TV downstairs was going at its volume's peak. Not only were the televisions screaming they were on a channel that we wouldn't dare watch. It was a children's channel, something our grandson, Jayveun, would watch. It could have been ICarly or something else just as unstimulating to the adult brain.

The Black Widow

The minute I descended the next set of stairs, I immediately started demanding an explanation. He was slumped in the rocking chair and he sort of stammered as he said that he didn't turn the televisions on. I was fit to be tied. At first I didn't really notice that something wasn't right, I was too caught up in myself and my agitation. As I stepped closer it was obvious that something was wrong. He didn't have his oxygen on and his clothing, I realized, was unchanged from the night before. As I narrowed the gap between us I noticed that his pants were wet and his shirt was half buttoned and damp from drool. Instantly my rage was gone, something was wrong with my baby. And as the song goes, *'when something is wrong with my baby something is wrong with me'.* It was now about 6:30a.m.

I extended my hands to help him from the chair. He was unsteady and had very little use of himself but I managed to get him upstairs and to the bathroom. All kinds of thoughts were racing through my head. One thing I thought was whether he could have had a stroke. I was also thinking about my MRI and the fact that I didn't know a number to call and cancel my appointment. After all it was Saturday and the normal office connections weren't available. But when I made the appointment the scheduler did say that it wouldn't take long, particularly since it was Saturday. I made the decision to keep my appointment. I woke Ashley, our daughter, briefed her and told her that her father was in the bathroom and to just be on the alert. J.W. told me that he'd stay put until I got back. I freshened up, dressed, grabbed my jacket and scurried to the Expedition, never even putting the jacket on. I made it to my appointment in about fifteen minutes, sobbing the whole way. I telephoned my mama, as I drove up the highway, to let her know what was going on and to wish her happy birthday. She was celebrating 94 years. Mama began trying to soothe and comfort me but my tears were relentless.

Finally, I was where I had to be and the MRI was underway. All I could think about

The Black Widow

as I lay there, tears dripping in my ears, was getting back home to my husband. Within the hour or slightly over I was back home and I immediately picked up where I had left off. Meanwhile he had managed to start trying to wash up. I took over and finished getting J.W. cleaned up and brushed his teeth. I got him to bed and a little breakfast in him. His appetite was scant. I probably should have insisted that we go to the hospital but he really didn't want to. At least he was comfortable. By the end of the day he was showing some signs of improving. He didn't eat much but I did manage to keep him fairly hydrated. He urinated constantly, not generally making it to the bathroom, so for the majority of the day I cleaned him, the bed and kept the washing machine going. But as I said by the end of the day he was doing better. At least his urine flow had calmed down.

It was about mid-afternoon when Jade, our youngest daughter, and Jayveun, her son, came to the house. Shortly after that Jade and Ashley went to the mall. Jayveun wanted to

Faye J. Williams

stay with PahPah. Jayveun and his grandfather were always very close. Around 4:30p.m. I went to Walgreens, leaving Jayveun and J.W. home alone, and purchased some disposable items, just in case. Thankfully I didn't have to use them. I was only going to be gone for a short while and Ashley and Jade were due back at any moment. It was decision time, however. I called John, my step-son, that night and brought him up to speed. I also told him that I wanted him to have keys to our home and the alarm system code, that way he could always enter our home easily and check on his father, especially since he worked second shift. By the next day he was still showing signs of continued improvement. I made him a doctor's appointment for the next week. Donna, my oldest step-daughter agreed to take him for the appointment. After a thorough exam and a battery of tests it was determined that he hadn't had a stroke and basically this event was brought on likely because of the extended time without his oxygen. The appointment was long and exhausting. The balance of December went okay but by January, 2012 a black cloud hovered over us once again. It made a crash landing on January 31st.

It was around 2:00 a.m. when J.W. rose from bed to go to the bathroom, waking me meanwhile, so I went to the bathroom as well. I had figured that by the time I was finished that he should also have been finished. I eased back into bed and waited for him to return. I asked him a couple of times if he was okay. He said that he was but I kept hearing an unusual sound coming from the bathroom. Finally, he asked me to come to him and when I opened the bathroom door, I gasped. He was in trouble. Every ounce of strength he possessed had gone down the toilet. He was hugging the sink and he had gotten so weak so quickly that he couldn't hold his head up any longer and it was drifting in and out of the sink which made the muffled sound that I kept hearing. Somehow I managed to get him to step back so that he could sit on the toilet and rest a minute. He tried to convince me that he was okay but he was trembling, he was scared and he was sick. He was not okay. After a few minutes I tried to help him stand so that maybe I could get him back to bed. It's amazing how quickly things can change. He walked into the bathroom but there was no way that he was going to walk out, even with my help. I summoned Ashley and she tried to help us but he slipped to the floor just the same. I had to call 911. Very shortly after that three men and a fire truck blazed up my street. They were so kind. Our bedroom isn't very large and they didn't have much room to maneuver but they got him back on the bed. They did a quick assessment, suggested that I contact his primary physician and then they left. Truly J.W. should have gone to the hospital then but he insisted that he'd be okay. I prayed for a miracle. With J.W. back in bed, I covered him up and rested my head on his shoulder until he drifted off to sleep.

By now, it's about 6:30. I called work and left a message on my supervisor's voice mail that I wouldn't be in. I telephone Dr.

The Black Widow

McCallie's office at 9:00 and she instructed me to bring him to the emergency room. J.W. really didn't want to go to the hospital but he knew that the decision was non-negotiable and non-debatable. I washed him up and helped him into some clean pajamas, his yellow happy face pajama pants and an oversized tee. I updated Mama, with the morning's events, and she told James, my brother-in-law. With a few hours of rest under his belt J.W. was able to walk, with lots of assistance, down the steps and to James' car. Off to the hospital we went.

    We are now at the hospital and registered. They immediately go to work on him, checking his vitals and starting an IV. His temperature was 100.5 and he was trembling quite a bit, his breathing was labored and his lungs weren't clear. After a battery of tests were taken and the results in, it was determined that he had aspirated pneumonia, I also heard it called aspiration pneumonia. This pneumonia occurs when swallowed food sometimes gets off the beaten path of the digestive system and veers into the lungs. He was also diagnosed with congestive heart failure. Needless to say I was scared. Once the necessary treatment was rendered, he improved rather quickly and was released on Friday, February 3rd. He was like a new man.

CHAPTER 2

The Fog Cleared

Now, although J.W. seemed to be 'out of the woods' his doctor had scheduled him for a few sessions of physical therapy to start on Sunday, February 5th. J.W. needed therapy to help strengthen his legs.

That morning, I was able to get him to eat a little and take his medication. The therapist arrived around 10:00 Sunday morning. She began by asking a set of questions very similar to those previously asked by medical personnel. A few of the questions were different and some were asked for verification. Because of his congestive heart failure diagnosis, I was supposed to weigh him each morning and give him a diuretic, to help rid his body of excess fluid, if his weight was above 2 pounds more than it was the day before. This particular morning J.W. was beginning to have problems again. He was weak and his tremors, because of the Parkinson's disease, were increasing. I only thought the fog had cleared, that the rough patches were behind us. I knew that it would take time to recover fully but I was very hopeful that we were on the road to recovery. Not so fast. Mary, the therapist tried unsuccessfully to get a reading on the scale. Then she decided to try to give him some bed exercises, again unsuccessful. Mary was not able to accomplish her purpose. J.W. was having trouble focusing and staying awake. Mary wasn't there very long because what she came for she couldn't do. Later that afternoon many friends from church and family called to check on him. My phone rang constantly. I was never bothered by the ringing phone because each call was a show of love and concern. Michael and Kellye Ludy and family came to visit that afternoon. Kellye had called before they came to see if we had eaten dinner because otherwise she was going to bring us dinner. Well, we hadn't eaten. Michael is our minister and when they arrived we had a short service in our bedroom. It was February but the weather was mild. The day was very clear and the sun was 'cuttin up' so their children were mostly outside playing basketball.

J.W.'s condition was constantly declining. Kellye fixed him a little food on a saucer but he wasn't able to eat anything. He was starting to drift off to sleep so we migrated to the living room. We had been seated only a few minutes when we heard a thud. Michael rushed upstairs, Kellye and I close behind. Michael told Kellye to call Kolbe, their oldest son. J.W. had fallen. My heart sank. Kolbe was a strapping young man of about 14 years of age. Michael and Kolbe lifted J.W. back on the bed like he was a loaf of bread. J.W.

was headed to the bathroom but he was too weak to make it. I cleaned him up, changed his clothes and helped him use the urinal. It was becoming more apparent, with each passing moment, that we weren't far from an emergency room visit. Around 4:30ish Michael, Kellye and family left. I continued to monitor his condition very closely. I couldn't put off the inevitable any longer. I called Anne & James (my sister and brother-in-law) and John and asked them to come to the house. I knew what I had to do and I needed some additional family by my side. By this time Ashley had returned home from evening church service. I tried to give J.W. his evening medication to no avail. He could only swallow the pills in his mouth but he didn't have the strength to swallow. This time there was no question as to whether he could be taken to the hospital by personal vehicle. Anne or Ashley called 911. I was busy hovering over J.W. and getting him ready for the hospital. His Parkinson's was nearly out of control; the shaking was terrible. That was actually the first time that I'd slipped the disposable underwear on him. He was so pitiful and I was also fighting back my enormous tears that I'd so far managed to keep at bay.

The ambulance was there in record time. As usual the personnel asked several questions; What's going on? How long has he been like this? What hospital are we going to? They checked his temp and vitals. They also asked J.W. a few questions just to check alertness and the answers were mostly incorrect. J.W. was lifted into a special chair and taken downstairs. From there he was transferred onto the gurney.

As we journeyed to the hospital, I made a few phone calls. One was to Mary Davenport, my dear friend and sister in Christ, who simply said, "I'll meet you at the hospital". I called a few other people who I knew would call others to update them. Once we arrived at the hospital, the person at the front desk said that he'd let us know something as soon as possible.

The Black Widow

The waiting room was crowded. A lot of folks had their eyes glued to the TV screen watching the Super Bowl. I have no idea who was playing except I kept hearing the name, Eli Manning, over and over again.

Finally, I was ushered to where my husband was. He was connected to an IV and his temp had spiked to 102. I telephoned those in the waiting room and brought them up to speed. The doctors, nurses and techs continued to work on him, drawing blood, checking monitors and attempting to engage him in conversation as much as possible. "Mr. Williams, how do you feel? What is your pain level? What year is this? To that he responded 2020… ...2020? That made me laugh. Who is the President? His answer was close, he said Obamarama. How many children do you have? He said "five". Now which one he left off, who knows. My family now joined me. J.W. was struggling and it was apparent he was a very sick man. Finally, after the medications started to kick in, his fever went down, and his tremors began to settle down some. Hours later he had settled into a hospital room and I was in a chair by his bed. J.W. was a totally new man. He was alert and aware of everything. He saw some recaps of the Super Bowl and he started educating me on the anatomy of football. I don't want to know about football on a good day. But just having him 'back' and talking to me I endured my lesson. I don't remember who Ashley and John were cheering for but that team won. Once again things are looking up. J.W. was able to walk again with little or no assistance.

    The days rocked on and on. I was becoming more familiar with Memorial Hospital than I wanted to be but that was our place of healing. Finally, the day came for him to be discharged. J.W. was discharged on February 10th but not for home. He was scheduled to be relocated to Siskin Rehabilitation Hospital. Of course that's not what he wanted to do but he made up in his mind, with some gentle encouragement, that for him to get the best quality of life from that point forward that he needed to learn some life skills and techniques that would promote just that. One particular concern Siskin would deal with was swallow therapy and another was physical therapy. His inability to swallow properly was likely because his Parkinson's disease was advancing. Many people with Parkinson's disease have difficulty swallowing because they lose control of their mouth and throat muscles.

CHAPTER 3

Room 257

It was nearly 5:00p.m. when the transport arrived to take J.W. to Siskin. He was loaded on a stretcher as I packed his personal items. I met them at the rehabilitation center. We arrived at Siskin at about the same time. J.W. was tired and winded when he got there but he was determined to do whatever it took so that he could come home to his family once again. He sat on the bed and patted the mattress. He said that it felt better than the bed at Memorial. He complained that the mattress at Memorial was heated. The mattress was not heated but it did inflate and deflate so that patients would be less likely to develop bed sores. I sat in a chair across from Tina, the admissions nurse, and completed his admissions paperwork. Once I got him settled, I left for home with the promise that I'd be back bright and early the next morning to help him get started for the day which would also include his first physical therapy session.

We had been having some cold days and some not too cold days but frigid temperatures were scheduled for the next several days. When I arrived home late that Friday evening, it was dark, and cold and I was hungry. The first thing that I did was start a fire in the wood stove. Ashley and Jade weren't comfortable handling the wood stove and I was okay with it because I wasn't keen on them burning themselves or burning the house down. I could already feel a difference in the temperature as I gathered wood from the side of the utility building. It was an icy cold starless night and on top of that the heat was out in the Expedition.

Faye J. Williams

    Saturday morning, February 11, 2012, at 6:30a.m. I am walking the halls of Siskin headed to room 257. J.W. is up and having breakfast and he's still looking pretty good. He said that he had a fair night. I helped him get washed up and changed and gathered the soiled laundry. I left about 7:45a.m. for my 8:00a.m. hair appointment with Thomas at Total Image. My plan was to return to Siskin once my appointment was over but J.W. insisted that I not come back because of the unfavorable weather prediction. That was one time that I truly obeyed my husband. He didn't have to twist my arm not one bit. I got my hair done, stopped at the store, came home and added wood to my fire and rested. Bear, a local barber and friend, visited him that afternoon and gave J.W. a beautiful haircut and shave. Now although we were very early in the rehab process, I was beginning to feel like there was a glimmer of hope, like J.W. was going to at least be restored to where he was before last December.

The Black Widow

When we talked about his hopes and our dreams he most often said that his wish and prayer were to get well so that he could, once again, be active in the church. He also wanted to relieve me of some of the pressure that he thought I was under. Granted, this was not an easy time for me but I always knew that our situation could be worse and a worse time was not very far away.

We are now into our third day at Siskin and so far, so good. It's Sunday morning and extremely cold. Before going to church I went to Siskin to make sure he was okay. When I arrived at church I parked directly in front of the building, in the direct sunlight. By the time church was over the Expedition was nice and toasty. Since I had already been to Siskin that morning, I opted to go later in the afternoon because several people from church were planning to visit him. By the end of the day Sunday, he was tired. On Monday he was back to his prescribed physical routine but he didn't feel well. Around Tuesday afternoon I got a call from Siskin on my cell phone letting me know that they had taken him to Erlanger Medical Center for tests. The tests that Erlanger would perform were akin to the ones at Siskin but a second opinion is always good. Besides had Erlanger discovered something that Siskin did not, he was at the right place for more advanced treatment. As it turned out he was dehydrated. Since his diagnosis of aspirated pneumonia, he was supposed to drink liquids with a thickening powder in it. Needless to say he wasn't consuming adequate fluids. As a result of the dehydration both Siskin and Erlanger concluded acute renal failure, this condition occurs when your kidneys suddenly become unable to filter waste products from your blood. The doctors also told me that he had fluid on his brain but that wasn't the big concern, the big concern was his kidneys. They further stated that the condition was reversible once they pumped fluids into him. So he was given two liters of fluid and once again he was a new man. I didn't mention his trip to Erlanger to anyone, I just finished my shift and afterward headed to Siskin, as always. When I left Siskin that night he was resting pretty good.

Because of so much going on with J.W. people were constantly calling to check on him. When I was home I always took my cell phone and landline phone with me all over the house, even to the bathroom, just so I wouldn't miss a call from friends, family or especially the hospital. This night, however, I let my guard down. It was only hours earlier that I left Siskin and he was doing pretty well. Around 11:00p.m. I was in the bathroom, without either phone. But thank God Ashley was home and she heard my cell phone ringing. It was Siskin and they had rushed my husband to Erlanger Medical Center. My heart sank to the pit of my stomach.

CHAPTER 4

When Something Is Wrong with My Baby...Something is Wrong with me

I dialed the number that Ashley had jotted down so that I could be told firsthand what was going on. I tried to stay calm, no matter the news. I didn't immediately rush to Erlanger, the caller said he would update me shortly. I sat a few minutes thinking the

The Black Widow

worse. I flipped the TV on and back off. My thoughts were on E. 3rd Street, the location where J.W. was fighting for his life. About ten minutes later the phone rang again. I was informed that his condition was not good and the decision had been made to admit him. I immediately dressed and headed to Erlanger. The night was black and freezing and so was the Expedition. I prayed as I drove first one street and then the other until finally I was there. I was able to park directly in front of the emergency entrance. I rushed to the information desk stating who I was and why I was there. My eyes slowly scanned the lobby while I awaited information about my husband. Several people dotted the lobby, a few security folks and several other people for as many reasons. I recognized one of the security men as the son of a church member. Magazines without covers, food wrappers and an abandoned beverage can, littered the waiting room. Honestly, the area was dirty but I did take a seat close to the double door that the lady vanished through to gather updated information about my husband. It still gets next to me how places of healing can be so obviously unclean.

Shortly, the woman emerged from the other side of the double door and told me that they were 'working on him'. I sat there feeling so helpless. I didn't call anybody, I just sat there, my mind wandering to the edge of night. I thought about the first time that we met, the times that he made me happy, the times that he ticked me off and praying that this wasn't the end because we still had some unfinished business. I thought about some of his favorite passages of scripture and one of my favorite songs, *"Precious Lord, take my hand lead me..."* My somber thoughts were interrupted, 'Are you Mrs. Williams?', asked a woman in a smock. I only nodded. She directed me through the double door, to my husband's side. Oh, Lord, was I unprepared for what was ahead. He only wore a hospital gown, a catheter was inserted and the area, the room, was filthy. There was a small container on the bed with gauze in it and a fair amount of blood, shaved or clipped pubic hair was on the floor as was empty wrappers of various paraphernalia. It was like a scene from an emergency room television show, uncut and uncensored. I didn't cry, I was in awe. I thought to myself, *how could this be happening?* His blood pressure had plummeted, he was lethargic and his breathing was shallow, very shallow.

The emergency room doctor explained the gravity of J.W.'s condition to me. He told me that J.W. had been given medication to raise his blood pressure but his breathing was very bad. I stood by his side, gently caressing his arm. Trying to understand and process all that I was being told. "*Mrs. Williams*", the doctor said, locking eye contact, *'If his breathing doesn't improve, we will have to put him on a ventilator'!* He stressed ventilator and he continued to say that if people in his condition are placed on a ventilator, they generally don't come off of it. He asked me repeatedly if I understood. Yes, I did understand. He meant that there could be, as my daddy used to say, *some slow walking and some sad singing*. I got it, I understood but I remained prayerful. J.W. tried to tell me something. His feet were uncovered and he was pointing downward. I covered his feet ...I could only guess that was what he was trying to tell me. I continued to stand vigil. His attachments hummed and beeped. Eventually I was escorted to the waiting area and was told that I'd be notified when he was in a room. He was going to be in the Medical Intensive Care Unit (MICU). It was 3:00 a.m.

The waiting area was dismal and pretty occupied. There were chairs and recliners and just enough light to manage not to bump into and trip over stuff. It was fairly quiet except for the snoring and the sound of people repositioning themselves in their recliners. I know that everyone has a story and I figured that each of the people in the room was very likely as on edge as I was. I also noticed a small office with uncovered windows. The lights were on in the office and there was a man in the office that had on a hoodie. It was hard for me to guess his age because of the hoodie. There was an empty chair near the office so I planted myself there and began my wait. There wasn't anything to do so I pulled pen and paper from my purse, gleaned as much light as possible from the office and made a few notes of what I was feeling. I felt scared and alone. The 'what-if' thoughts jumped around in my head like fleas. I had only been writing and pondering a short while when the man from the office came to me and asked who I was waiting for. It was only then that I knew that he wasn't a young man. I told him who I was there regarding and he said that he thought he knew J.W. from the Westside community. He introduced himself as Robert Bailey. He then excused himself and said that he'd return momentarily. Robert went back to his office and called the nurses' station to inquire about J.W. He must have been told that they didn't have a J.W. because I overheard Robert say, *"I think it's James".* I piped up and said 'John ...it's John'. Robert completed his call and told me that he was in bed 6 in MICU on the 7th floor.

I made a friend that night. I never felt that God had abandoned me, rather He continued to put people in my path, to calm my fears and anxieties. As Robert guided me to J.W. I tried to focus on wall art and other distinguishable characteristics along the way. Robert talked to me about the Westside, about Erlanger being the best hospital in the city and about the quality of care that J.W. was receiving. Of course, Robert was biased because he was a retired nurse from Erlanger. Robert told me that he thought J.W. was a little older than he and he was right. When I first saw Robert in his office, I could not tell anything about him because of the hoodie but as we walked and talked it became clear to me that he was an older man twilighting two worlds. Robert told me that he was 73, J.W. was 74. I learned a lot about Robert as we made our way to J.W.'s room. As we walked the halls of the hospital, we encountered several of Robert's comrades. One man, for instance, spoke to Robert and asked him how he was doing, to which Robert responded, "I'm cool". Another time just as we made it to J.W.'s room Robert acknowledged someone by tilting his head upward, *"What's up?"* I was so thankful to Robert for his kindness. I know that God truly puts people in our path when we need them the most. My path was dark for sure but God...but God speckled the dark walkway with beacons of light along the way.

    I was finally there with the love of my life. I stroked his hand but he was never the wiser. J.W. was sedated and unaware of my presence. It was nearly 5:00a.m. Because of the prescribed visiting hours in MICU, I decided, after spending a few minutes with him, that I'd go home and prepare for work. I only had five weeks of vacation time and I was rapidly using it, so whenever there was an opportunity to preserve a little, I grabbed it. There was no way for me to predict what lay ahead and the time it would require. The one thing that I did know was that my time

Faye J. Williams

was J.W.'s time and if it ran out, God would provide. I had to work and I had to take care of my husband and the rest would work itself out. As I drove home, I telephoned John and updated him. When I arrived home I texted my friend Sharron and called Anne and James to give them an update of the morning's events. The tears that I had managed to keep at bay finally broke through. I cried relentlessly. Ashley overheard me and came in the kitchen where I was, her eyes were red from crying. Ashley updated Jade, our youngest daughter. I went on to work. Once I arrived my co-workers inquired of his condition and I told them everything that I knew. I also worked it out with management so that I could take lunch at 3:30p.m. while he was in MICU so that I could make the 4:00p.m. visitations. That afternoon when I got to the hospital, I was a little early and I looked up and there was Lisa, my youngest step-daughter, what a pleasant surprise. We walked in together and to our amazement he was doing a lot better. The big mask that had nearly completely

The Black Widow

covered his face was gone and he only had the nasal oxygen. He had been through such a difficult time and he was still fuzzy. Lisa and I had been there a few minutes when he looked at her and said, 'Are you Lisa?' We laughed. Lisa had been through so much herself. Her ordeal with Courtney's medical crises, wasn't over but certainly things were looking up. Courtney is Lisa's daughter. Ashley and Jade had visited earlier in the day. It was approaching 5:00p.m. when Lisa and I left. John came later that night. God continued to lift J.W. from the depths of despair and by the end of the week he was a new man, again. His eating had improved and his thoughts were once again clear. Except for the shower that he insisted that he'd had everything that he said was pretty much spot on. He told me several times about the shower and how good it felt. I never believed that he'd had a shower but he insisted and I would not have dared rob him of a pleasant memory, even if it was a dream.

Faye J. Williams

Many times over I rehearsed my wedding vows internally and each time the words rang truer and truer. Right now I was dealing with the, in sickness and in health part. I vowed a vow many years earlier and as God is my witness and help, I would always be by J.W.'s side. I felt blessed to have J.W. as my husband and friend. I was fully aware that into each life a little rain must fall and at the time we were experiencing a monsoon. I also continued to bear in mind that we serve a sovereign God, a loving God, a faithful God and a God that won't burden us with more than we can withstand. 1 Corinthians 10:13 ~ *There hath no temptation taken you but such as is common to man; but God is faithful, who will not suffer you to be tempted above that ye are able; but will with the temptation also make a way to escape, that ye may be able to bear it.*

CHAPTER 5

Starting All Over Again

Even though J.W. had only been away from Siskin a short while, returning was like starting all over again. The only thing that had remained the same was the room. So the registrar shoots me a battery of questions and I routinely spit out the answers. She continues to make entries into the computer and periodically looks at J.W. I am now being asked about his allergies and ailments. I took her back to his previous hospitalizations and his first admission to Siskin. Before I'd named all of his ailments, she asked if he had Sleep Apnea, she had been observing his breathing. When I told her about his Parkinson's disease and how his shakes are so violent at times she told me something that I flat didn't know. What I learned was that anytime the body is insulted or assaulted by some other illness or sickness the Parkinson's acts out of control like a bad child, causing severe shakes. Well, do tell! I started to think back and it made so much sense because the times he had gone to Memorial Hospital he did have a fever and his tremors were through the roof. Over the next several days and weeks, he slipped into a routine of physical therapy, speech therapy and swallow techniques. Grant it, the road to recovery or stability wasn't easy but thank God, no more emergency trips to the hospital. He continued to fight vigorously to ascertain mental and physical integrity. Scores of well-wishers visited with him and often called to check on him. Finally, on March 1st, Gail Peterson, a caseworker at Siskin, called me and briefed me on their previous Thursday's staff meeting regarding J.W.'s progress. I

Faye J. Williams

was told that he was doing well, however, he would need 24/7 care once he was released. I wasn't prepared for that. I sucked in a deep breath, not knowing what to say. I really thought that his improvement was better than that. Once I settled the facts in my mind, I was better able to process the next steps. According to Gail his cognitive skills were a concern. Well we had managed bigger hurdles than that, and I believed the Lord would provide. Inpatient therapy was to continue for another week and a half. A release date was scheduled for March 10th and afterward he'd continue therapy at home. For the next several days J.W. continued to work hard and make reasonable progress. As his final days at Siskin drew nigh, several people stopped by his room to wish him well. One man even told him that he thought J.W. was a 'goner' referring to his last rush to the hospital.

Finally, the day arrived for my husband to come home. It was a very sunny, warm day. Anne drove me to Siskin to pick him up because it would be easier for him to get in a car as opposed to the high-stepping Expedition and John met us at the house to help his father navigate from the car to the house. I held my breath when J.W. walked up the steps but John was close behind to make sure he was safe. All went well. J.W. often commented about the beautiful day and how thankful he was to be home. Mary and another dear friend, Sarah, prepared and delivered dinner to us and several folks called to make sure that we were okay. J.W. was pretty weak and he tired very easily. His voice, once strong, baritone and steady was now unsure and unsteady but at least he was home. When we went to bed that night, we held hands and prayed to God thanking Him for that moment in time. We had so much to be thankful and grateful for.

We had a long road ahead but as always we would sojourn together.

CHAPTER 6

Home Sweet Home...Or Not

I didn't want to accept that he needed as much care as he did but I soon realized that the professionals at Siskin actually knew more than I did...lol. I prayed hard and I even stood at church one Sunday and asked the congregation to pray for me that I wouldn't become weary in well-doing. Yes, I was tired but so what, so was J.W. I started saying things to him like, '*Hey, do you need anything else while I'm in the kitchen? Can I get something for you before I sit down? If*

The Black Widow

you want something special from the store, please write it down. ...I can't remember everything, What else can I do for you?', I will be there in just a minute ... I was just trying to save a few steps for myself. Invariably he'd remember something or think of something after the fact. It was a constant Faye this and Faye that ...Faye, Faye, Faye. Sometimes for me to just be able to sit alone in the kitchen and nurse a steaming hot cup of Maxwell House was all I needed to be rejuvenated, refreshed and renewed. But as time moved on and he gained more confidence he eventually stabilized to the degree that he could actually do a lot for himself.

People used to ask me if I was taking care of myself...eating and sleeping properly. The short answer was, no, but it was okay. What wasn't okay was how I was feeling. You can't say everything to everybody but blessed is the caregiver that has friends that can be trusted, friends that won't think harshly of you just because you need to 'sound-off' every now and again. I cried to a friend one day how pleased I was that J.W. was doing so well but of all things I was feeling angry because he wasn't totally dependent on me anymore. Of all things. How dare I feel that way! I don't remember what she said or if she said anything, I just know that once I verbalized my thoughts, I felt better. Maybe angry wasn't the right word to use. He no longer needed me for absolutely everything and for that I should have been happy.

Weeks drifted by and he did gain strength but not to the point that he could drive or gather the garbage or do chores, even though he did try. I continued to watch him closely, sometimes from a safe distance because I never wanted him to feel smothered.

Finally, one of his most fervent prayers was answered. He was back at church, which was a major blessing. Not only was he happy to see everyone but they were equally glad to see him. He wanted so much to let the congregation know how much he appreciated the love and concern shown to us during his illness and convalescence. He stood and expressed his gratitude...his genuine, absolute, thankfulness. His voiced cracked but he made it through.

Time continued to rock on and he continued to be on the uptick. Doctor's visits, sure, but no hospitalizations. Considering all of the dark days behind us and his 75th birthday was on the horizon, I thought of how fitting it would be to celebrate it with a surprise birthday party. J.W. had an appointment with his primary physician on July 30th and she told him how well he was doing and that he'd 'cheated death' early on. We didn't buy into the 'cheating death' theory because there's no way to override God's grace. God just wasn't ready to reel him in yet.

I know how right it is not to take anything for granted but through prayer and supplication are we able to do anything that we do. I prayed often and thanked God often for His many blessings. I also prayed that

God would bless my endeavor to celebrate his birthday. Party plans were made and executed and everything went well. I could not have pulled it off successfully had it not been for some very faithful friends and loved ones. The party was held at the church and it was my job to get him there. I don't remember what I told him that we had to go to church for but whatever I said, he accepted. We were a little delayed because I'd stopped by Walgreens before picking him up from home and inadvertently locked my keys in our vehicle and had to wait for help. When we finally arrived he noticed the many cars on the lot but he didn't comment or ask any questions. We opened the back entrance of the church and everyone sang Happy Birthday to him. He was still weak but I was able to steady him. It turned out to be a lovely day and he was so overjoyed. We had been through so much and were extremely thankful to everyone who continued to remember us in prayer. I took a few moments during the party to recognize two particular people who had truly been a rock to me during this time. I recognized John with a 'hero' trophy and Mama with a 'shero' trophy. They both deserved them so much. We took lots of pictures and had a wonderful time. We talked about the party weeks after it was over. No matter how good times were, we remained prayerful and hopeful for even better days.

One Sunday morning in January of 2013, J.W. stood before the congregation and read the scripture which was taken from Luke, chapter 2. His voice quivered, but he did it. Always with the assistance of his cane, he ascended and descended the two steps to the podium with relative ease. He also became stable enough to work with the wood burner again on a limited basis.

Life certainly wasn't without its challenges but our faith in the Great I Am, continued to sustain us.

Even with improved health I tried not to leave J.W. alone too often. I had to work but I tried to run errands around the schedules of others as much as possible. I really tried to encourage J.W. to be careful and mindful of his limitations. He tried but sometimes he was a little careless. Like the morning the fire had extinguished from the wood burner. J.W. fiddled with it and then he went back upstairs. When I opened the wood burner door it was only slightly smoking. It appeared to me that the ashtray needed emptying. Normally when I'd empty the ashtray I would use a steel rod to search the top, bottom and sides of the chamber to clear away the debris. The debris would fall through the grate into the ash tray and I'd empty as much as possible at that particular time. When I tried to do so I realized that J.W. had stuffed it with newspaper. Well he said that since he couldn't move the large piece of wood inside the wood burner to place a fire log under it that he would stuff the bottom of the wood burner and ignite the paper so that the flames would rise through the grate and burn better. Maybe that wasn't the best idea. I thought that was a recipe for disaster. So I used the rod to pull the paper

The Black Widow

out of the ashtray and as I did remnants of paper was still burning but quickly extinguished when it hit the hearth. Then came a larger hunk of paper that was actually burning. I tried to pull it from the ashtray and quickly toss it inside the wood burner but I dropped it instead, luckily on the hearth. The flames grew bigger and bigger. Had the paper fallen on the carpet I would have had a big problem. The house filled with smoke so badly that I had to open the back door to help de-smoke the house. Finally, thank God, the paper burned itself out. J.W. tried to assist but I encouraged him to go back upstairs. The last thing he needed was to inhale the smoke. Everything worked out.

CHAPTER 7

J. W., Please Work with Me

J.W. grew impatient with himself at times but I reminded him that if he did something that was unnecessary and it proved to be to his detriment, that he would not be the only one to suffer from his actions. Sometimes when the kids were home with him and I was out running errands he would flex his parental status and do things his way, even when they suggested that he not.

One such day in February of 2013, I had left home to run errands before the weather took a turn for the worse. It was very cold and grey with snow flurries predicted. Jade, Ashley and Jayveun were there with J.W. I had already gone to Kinko's to copy the church bulletin and from there I went to Walmart. While in Walmart the snow started to fall. It came down quickly and piled up quickly. As I stood in the check-out line my cell phone rang. It was Jayveun calling to tell me that PahPah had driven off in the Expedition to have the tires checked. I honestly couldn't believe what I was hearing. Of all days, with snow on the ground plus he hadn't been driving and no one needed the Expedition. I had bought a new car in the fall of 2012. Why, on earth, would he do such a foolish thing? Anger quickly washed over me like a wave but I wasn't there and I'm sure that they did everything possible to prevent J.W. from going but he went anyway. I was very angry, but there wasn't a darn thing that I could do about it. I was in Walmart, in line to be checked out. So I took several deep breaths in an attempt to calm myself. The anger dissipated. I told Jayveun that I was sure they'd done everything possible to dissuade him from leaving and that all we could do at that point was pray for his safe return and that no harm would come to him or anyone else. That proved to be a short, stupid trip. God blessed him to get back home safely. By the time I returned home the snow had stopped and the streets were clear again. I must admit, I was ticked off at him for that selfish stunt of his. I was angry and afraid for what could have happened.

Every day in our household was not Sunday by any means. We didn't hurl hurtful words at one another. That was something that we just never did. When I needed a break from J.W., I would involve myself in yard work or housework or writing. When he needed a break from me he'd sit on the patio and bird watch, if the weather permitted. If it wasn't good for him to go outside or if he didn't feel like it, he would watch back to

The Black Widow

back episodes of In The Heat of The Night or a series of westerns or whatever was on TV. Mostly though, the television would watch him. He generally fell asleep very soon after sitting down.

    I tried not to be pessimistic about his well-being and his progress but I saw him each and every day and the truth was, he was no longer improving. Not only was he not improving, but he also wasn't even holding his own. I was beginning to notice a decline in his health. Sometimes he couldn't complete a thought, other times he'd drift off during a conversation. He had been experiencing severe pain and swelling in his legs and feet for quite some time and the only thing that brought him relief from the pain was ibuprofen. I bought large bottles of ibuprofen and he took large dosages along with his prescribed meds. He continued to get up early each morning because he said that lying in bed after about 5:00a.m. made his back hurt. We continued to pray fervently, thanking God and asking Him for better days. He also developed worsening problems swallowing and his hands tremored more. He insisted that I buy the thickening agent that he used at Siskin to help him swallow better. I did but it didn't help. The problems swallowing and the subsequent drooling were part of the Parkinson's as it advanced.

CHAPTER 8

The Fall of a Tower

There's a certain amount of integrity and pride that keeps a man standing. But when that integrity and pride are constantly being chipped away, little by little, brick by brick he cannot continue to endure. J.W. worked hard to follow the doctors' instructions. He wanted so desperately to get better. He would, sometimes, get ideas from watching, **The Doctors**, and he'd have me going to the store for this or that. And I'd usually do whatever he said. One of his doctors suggested that J.W. take physical therapy to strengthen his legs. I don't recall which doctor told him that but I went along with it, even though I thought that his COPD was much too severe to tolerate physical therapy. So off, like a prom dress, we went to Benchmark Rehabilitation, for physical therapy. After the first couple of sessions my husband said that he felt better. I was cautiously optimistic.

I constantly urged him to be careful and not to overdo it. And he tried. I watched him when he didn't know I was watching. He would say in one breath that he wasn't going to worry about his health, that it was all in God's hands. Then in the next breath he would say, 'M*an, I wish I knew what was causing this. This don't make sense. Imo call my doctor tomorrow, somebody gone tell me something. All these doctors and can't nobody tell me nothing!"* Sometimes I didn't know what to say. I'd squeeze his hand gently or just hold him close. Other times I'd just listen.

The days and months crept on and Kitten, our youngest granddaughter was now seven months old and faster than greased lightning. On Saturday evening, February 15th J.W. was sitting in a chair at the kitchen table and Kitten was speeding around in her walker. A few times she got close to the steps but there wasn't any danger of her falling because her mother and auntie were standing close by. A time or two J.W. reached for her because he thought she was teetering too close for comfort. I was washing dishes and I told him that she was fine. Well he reached for her yet again and this time he more than outreached his range and he fell out of the chair. He fell hard. After a few minutes he was able to pull himself up. He totally misjudged the distance. And yes it angered me because he didn't need to fall, especially one such fall as that, an unnecessary fall. Unfortunately, that was only the beginning. On Monday, February 17th, he was messing with the wood burner, lost his balance and banged his fragile body on the floor. Again nothing broken. The very next night, February 18th around 8:30p.m., I was sitting

The Black Widow

in bed holding our sleeping granddaughter, when suddenly I heard a terrible crash. *Oh, Lord, I prayed not again ...* I handed Kitten to Ashley and checked on J.W. This time he had gotten up to go to the bathroom. By now he feels the walls and door frames and tables or whatever is handy as he toddles along. This time, as before, he misjudged the distance. As he reached for the bookcase, he lost his balance and fell very hard. He wasn't hurt but he was very nervous. I encouraged him to sit there for a few minutes to gather himself. I sat on the floor with him. This time getting up proved to be a real challenge. I stepped in front of him to try to secure his hands and feet. Finally, I suggested that he get on his knees. After a few minutes, he managed to get up. Soon after that I helped him prepare for bed.

There are some things in life that we expect to change. The seasons know for sure which one follows the other, birds know how to strategize formations and take flight elsewhere, those are expectations. But I never expected my relationship with my husband, my tower of power, to take on such a new meaning. It's not just husband and wife anymore, it's now husband and wife/caregiver. It's these kinds of things in life that bring out the strength that we all have within. It reminds me of the old saying, *"Those things that don't kill us will make us stronger"*. There was a time when I tried to ignore certain things but like it or not reality was beginning to slap me hard. I prayed fervently to God for strength and guidance. Some thoughts I tried to keep to myself but when people would ask about him my eyes would often fill with tears.

The next few weeks were filled with more of the same, except, no more falls, thank goodness.

It is now mid-March and I took today off work to take J.W. to a doctor's appointment. His vitals were good and his heart rate was good, his weight was 230. Follow up appointments were scheduled with a podiatrist and a speech therapist for a swallow test, and an eye doctor.

The Black Widow

J.W. was having problems with tearing and the drooling was worsening. It was important that I accompanied him to this appointment so that I could get answers first hand. Besides I'm not with him at every appointment so when I am, I need to maximize the trip. Now for the follow-up appointments I could rely on Jade and James to help out.

CHAPTER 9

The Graduation

What a wonderful time. Ashley had worked so hard to earn her Master's Degree. It was an exciting, beautiful, sunny Saturday. J.W. wasn't raising any sand. He was kind of slowing down. There weren't any new health issues on the horizon. He was beginning to tire more easily. It was fair to say that he was doing just okay. I had been busy preparing everything that Ashley wanted for her reception that was going to be at Mama's house. She wanted bar-b-que and the fixings.

The Black Widow

Now, I didn't make the actual graduation, I stayed behind to get everything in order. Plus, I knew that J.W. couldn't go and I didn't want to leave him alone too long. As I prepared to take things to Mama's home I asked him if he felt like going. I even told him that if he decided to go and after a while felt tired that I would bring him home at any point. But I did tell him early on that this would be a long, exhausting day. He thought about it, but finally decided that he'd stay home…just for me to make sure that I brought him a plate. No problem. I would do that anyway.

Nearly everyone on the guest list was able to attend and every inch of the reception pleased her. J.W.'s absence was noticed but everyone knew that he wasn't well. I remember clearing one of the last tables as the evening was drawing to an end and Ashley eased close to me and kissed me on the cheek and thanked me. That was wonderful and I could tell that she was pleased. Not only had Ashley received her Master's Degree, a couple of months earlier she had landed a permanent job with Blue Cross-Blue Shield and she was in the process of preparing to move into her first apartment.

One of the things that I had planned to do the following week was work in the yard. All kinds of lovely flowers were popping from the earth, not to mention the accompanying weeds. There was mowing to be done and annuals to set in pots. Even though J.W. couldn't do any of the work, he could enjoy the fruits of my labor. He noticed everything, down to the single blade of grass that I missed once.

CHAPTER 10

Thank You, Lord

We hardly made it to Sunday school anymore because it would take him so long to get dressed, even with my help. Once he got up and took his prescription medication and some ibuprofen he would generally start to feel a little better. After breakfast, he had to rest a few minutes before he was able to shave. I would help him with his bath and help him dress. Sometimes we were blessed with a Sunday morning casserole that Teresa, John's beautiful girlfriend, would make and John would bring to us. Usually we would be done with breakfast but it would heat up nicely and we would have it for dinner.

Our drive to church was fairly quiet, a few remarks about the beautiful weather but mostly we were in our individual worlds, a Mighty Clouds of Joy cd played the distance. I listened to the selection, "Hold On" over and over again, the words were very soothing. By the end of the day he was completely worn out.

J.W. had an appointment with the podiatrist and a physical therapist for Monday morning but I canceled both. He was just too weak. As I prepared to go to work, I strongly urged him to just take it easy, to rest as much as possible. And he assured me that he would try. I called home to check on him around 11:30 but the phone only rang. I reasoned that maybe he was in the bathroom and just forgot to take the phone with him. I called again around an hour later, the same thing. I was beginning to get a little uneasy. I made plans to leave work at 1:30. Meanwhile, he called me. When he told me that he had fallen about two hours earlier, my heart sank. He had fallen in our bedroom as he tried to go to the bathroom. The phone was on the bed and it had just then crossed his mind to pull the cover toward him so that the phone could drop to the floor. And to make it worse, he still hadn't been able to get up. I told him that I was calling James to come help him but he insisted that he could get up. Two hours and he hadn't been able to get up. His voice sounded pretty good and he really did not want me to call for help. He assured me that while he was on the floor he did rest some; that he hadn't been struggling for two straight hours. I gave him an hour, but thanks be to God, he called me back in about twenty minutes. He had managed to get up and was back on the bed, but I still left work early. When I got home he was exhausted and hungry and damp - not too bad for the day that he had had. I gave him a bed bath, helped him put on some fresh pajamas, changed the linen and fixed him something to eat. By the end of the day he seemed okay, considering all.

The Black Widow

As the week wore on soreness set in and he complained a little about his chest hurting. I thought that likely he had pulled some unused muscles. Any mention of going to the hospital, however, was totally dismissed. But I watched him very closely. I watched and I prayed. I no longer knew what to pray for, only that God's will be done. I knew that God held us in the palm of His hand and I trusted Him completely. I no longer made any serious plans about anything because any and everything that I did was conditional, simply based on how J.W. was feeling at the time.

Springtime brought with it lots of showers and needless to say, the grass was inching higher and higher. Part of my weekend plan was to mow the lawn. Finally, early Saturday the rain stopped. Even before going outside to do yard work I would first make sure that J.W. was okay. Usually when I'd go outside he would monitor me to make sure that I took water breaks and stayed hydrated.

Faye J. Williams

Finally, late Saturday afternoon, I was able to mow the lawn. When I came inside all I wanted to do was take a nice relaxing bubble bath. I must have been in the tub an hour. When I finally surfaced, Jayveun asked me why was the floor downstairs wet. I wasn't for sure but I had to go and find out, plus Jayveun said that it was a lot of water. I was downstairs looking around when I heard a toilet flush and a gush of water poured from a pipe behind the washing machine. *No, not the plumbing!* I squealed. Yes, it was the plumbing. By now it's after 10:30, too late to do anything or call anybody. Plus, I was extremely tired and disgusted. What's the old saying, 'when it rains, it pours'. And it does...but God. But God knows our troubles and our needs. I put down some big, thick towels and went to bed.

The next morning, Mother's Day, we did manage to go to church. Afterwards we picked up a bucket of chicken and fixings from KFC. Once I got J.W. settled I phoned Roto Rooter Plumbing and Drain Cleaning

The Black Widow

Services to have the plumbing issue taken care of. When the serviceman arrived a few hours later J.W. insisted on going outside and showing him where Roto Rooter had made a repair about six months earlier. I pleaded with J.W. not to go outside, that I could show him. I insisted that J.W. sit on the nearby exercise bench because I was afraid that otherwise he would lose his balance. Just as J.W. bent his frail, feeble body to do as I had asked, he missed the bench by a hair and hit the floor. With only a little assistance he was able to get up. Once the plumbing was fixed and the serviceman left, J.W. told me that he was hungry. No problem. My plan was to fix him some dinner and then start the big task of cleaning up downstairs. Fortunately, the mess was only downstairs. I fixed his dinner and gave him the choice of coming to the kitchen or I could take his dinner to him. He chose to come to the kitchen. His steps were very slow. He managed to get to the kitchen sink to wash his hands. Meanwhile I had turned to clean the stove. All of a sudden I heard a terrific crash, he had fallen. I jerked around and exclaimed, "What happened?" He told me that he had turned to go to the table, after washing his hands, and he grabbed the back of the chair and the chair shifted and he lost his balance. What a hard fall that was because he was in a standing position and fell on the ceramic tile floor. Again, nothing was broken, and he was able to get up with my help. I took the next day off work to monitor him and to complete my clean-up.

The balance of the week was slow, no more falls at least. After I got off work, Thursday, May 15th and ran several errands, I decided after dinner to go ahead and give J.W. a haircut just in case we had to go to the hospital over the weekend. It is now Sunday, May 18th. We did not make it to church, he was too weak. I gave him his breakfast in bed. As usual he talked to several of his cousins and brothers later that day but he was tired. I knew that he was weary but he tried to stay positive. After all of our years of matrimony, he still kept me shut out of some of his private thoughts. And over the years, I accepted that. Lately he would say things to me that I would try to dismiss because there was a deeper meaning behind some of what he said. He said to me once, "Faye, I'm getting old". And on two separate occasions he said, "Faye, I'm old".

What he was really saying is that I was going to have to finish our journey without him. I could hardly stand to hear that. He would put his thin, cool hand on mine and hold it there briefly. Often he told me how much he loved me and really appreciated me. Tears would well up in my eyes. In my heart I knew J.W. was losing ground but by the same token I remained prayerful. I knew that his body could not continue to sustain the assaults that it was taking. I knew that in my heart. I also knew, '...but God'. But God was still on the powerful throne.

God, I knew, was still in the blessing business. Often, I'd check the mailbox only to find that some sweet soul had sent me a card with beautiful words of encouragement or someone had sent J.W. a card. Neighbors would often ask about him and tell me that they were lifting us up in prayer.

Monday, May 19th was just a fair day for J.W. He never changed from his pajamas. When I came in from work, I fixed his dinner and he managed to come in the kitchen to eat. As I was washing dishes I kept hearing his utensils clacking against his plate. I offered assistance but he insisted that he could manage. He told me that the chicken was kind of 'tough' though. I said 'okay'. Now I know that I'm no kitchen magician but I didn't really think that the chicken was tough. The next evening, I cooked the other piece of chicken that was in the package. Same thing. I fixed his plate, he came to the table and as he was eating, I was washing dishes. Often we didn't sit at the dinner table together because I always had several things to do and I didn't want my chores to get behind. I continued to hear his utensils clacking against the plate. This time I didn't offer assistance, I dried my hands and cut the chicken up for him. This time he claimed that the knife was dull. He was also having trouble balancing the peas with his fork, so I gave him a spoon instead. He remarked, 'glad I thought of that'. We both sort of laughed. The large majority of the clacking had to do with his Parkinson's because his tremors were getting worse and he didn't have much strength in his hands. That combination made it difficult to hold his silverware, let alone cut the meat.

That night he went to bed before I did but when I got up around 10:00p.m. to go to the bathroom he had gotten up and was in Jayveun's room. When Jade and Jayveun moved out a few years earlier I turned the empty room into Jayveun's room, that way when he visited he had his own space. Anyway, I suggested that he come back to bed and he promised that he would shortly. I went back to bed. I didn't wake up again until the clock alarmed at 4:00 a.m. I stretched my right arm to his side of the bed and felt nothing. I quickly sat up realizing that he evidently never came to bed. I pounced to Jayveun's room and, *oh my Lord,* he had fallen to the floor and was on his knees trying to get up. His shirt was wet from drool. Oh my God. I couldn't get him up, not even with Ashley's assistance. I called 911 for help.

Sirens screamed up Pine View Lane as emergency personnel answered my plea for help. The emergency folks lifted J.W. into a chair but I asked them if they'd put him in bed, which they so kindly did. One of the men asked a few questions about his condition and suggested that I contact his primary physician as soon as possible.

I had a lot of things going on. First and foremost was taking care of my husband. I also needed to be careful about my vacation time. Instead of sometimes taking a full day, I would use floating hours and leave work early. J.W. was finally resting in bed and I figured that after the morning he'd had that he would likely sleep a while. I decided to go to work but would leave early since he did have a doctor's appointment at 2:30p.m.

already scheduled. This appointment was with a new doctor concerning his heavy drooling.

As was my plan I clocked out at 1:30 and rushed home to help him get ready. After I had got home I wasn't pleased with the way he looked. I called the doctor's office and canceled the appointment, all the while thinking that maybe he needs to go to the emergency room. Meanwhile, I glanced sharply at the clock on the dresser, 2:15 p.m. I dialed Dr. Shannon McCallie's office, his primary physician, only to get the answering machine. I left a detailed message, of how he appeared to me, but didn't expect a call back because the greeting said something about calls received after 2:00p.m. may not be answered until the next day ...*I don't have until the next day.* I was a little disappointed but busied myself washing him up because I knew that an emergency room visit was in our very near future. Moments later the phone rang, it was Dr. McCallie's office. Based on the information that I'd left on their answering machine and the answers to the questions that the nurse asked her assessment was the same as mine…get to the emergency room. J.W. was past a rebuttal but he was a little hungry. After I had got him cleaned up, fresh pajamas on and brushed his teeth, he felt better. Even if he did accuse me of scrubbing too hard. I fixed him a sandwich and a little coke. While he ate I called James and asked him to come and help me take J.W. to the hospital. He said that he would be there in about thirty minutes. Perfect. J.W. only ate a couple of bites of his sandwich and told me to put the balance in a sandwich bag and take it with us. I packed his sandwich, a honey bun, his medication and a few other things in a travel bag and waited on James to arrive.

When James arrived he was able to get J.W. down the steps and in our car and off we went. We arrived at Memorial Hospital and was signed in around 5:00p.m. The sun was still shining brightly. I thought the lobby seemed rather busy for a Wednesday evening.

Later, as we waited to be summoned to complete our registration, I let Mary know where we were and that we wouldn't be attending Bible Class. I promised to update her later. I also instructed Ashley to text Donna, Lisa and John. And I was certain that one of the siblings would update Veronica, my step-daughter in Lynchburg, VA. Time ticked on but not too much before a slender lady, with a clipboard, emerged from a small office and announced, "John Williams".

We answered a battery of questions and was later ushered to an examination room to be checked out by a physician on call.

There, the hook-ups started. An IV, monitors and other paraphernalia to help the doctors determine J.W.'s condition. We were concerned with the things that we were familiar with; lungs, COPD, Sleep Apnea, diabetes, Parkinson's disease. That maybe one of these ailments had climbed to a new dimension. But when the doctor said that they were trying to determine if he'd had a heart attack, we were floored. Heart attack? I didn't know that there were values of determining if one had suffered a heart attack. We were told that by previous values a heart attack would have been ruled out but according to current values, yes J.W. had had a heart attack at some point. My mind immediately raced back to recent falls and how he had complained that his chest hurt, particularly following the fall when he scrambled on the floor for a couple of hours. After several hours of testing and awaiting results, it was determined that he'd be admitted for overnight observation. While the admission process was being finalized my hungry husband polished off his sandwich.

It was approaching 10:00p.m. when J.W. was finally in a room. I made sure that he was comfortable. It was a nice room. He was tired. We talked some but nothing special. Around 11:00p.m. the door eased open. It was Donna, Lisa and John. J.W. was so happy to see them. It was a very good visit. Lisa even fed J.W. a little bit of Jell-O. I think he talked more over the next hour than he had over the previous several hours. They left just after midnight and I left about an hour later. My drive home was quiet. The streets were clear.

The Black Widow

I listened to "Hold On", by The Mighty Clouds of Joy all the way home.

CHAPTER 11

Good Bye My Sweet Love, Good Bye My Friend

About 2:30a.m. the phone rang. It was the hospital calling. I had only been in bed about thirty minutes. J.W.'s condition had drastically deteriorated and he had been moved to the Cardio Vascular Intensive Care Unit (CVICU). His oxygen level and something else had dropped significantly. I was given a lot of information, it was overwhelming. The doctor rattled off the prescribed visitation hours and some other information but the first visitation wasn't until 8:30 a.m. About an hour later, it was the hospital again. This time the doctor wanted to be briefed on J.W.'s ailments and what exactly prompted me to bring him to the hospital.

Early Thursday morning, a few short hours after my second call from the hospital, I was up getting ready to return to Memorial Hospital. I drove to the hospital as quickly as I could. "Hold On" played over and over" Hold *on, you just hold on, well, well, well, well ...God will see you through".* I walked into his room and gasped. There J.W. was deeply sedated and on a ventilator. A hum or two here and beep or two there and other attachments that made no noise, he was catheterized and there was a tube down his throat. Family and friends were brought up to speed regarding his condition. When the sedation was less J.W. would respond by squeezing your hand. Not only were the

Faye J. Williams

visiting hours prescribed so was the length of time per visit.

On May 22nd J.W. had an echocardiogram, a test that uses high-frequency sound waves to make pictures of the heart and on May 23rd a heart catheterization, a procedure used to diagnose and treat some heart conditions. Both procedures yielded none positive results. He was definitely not a candidate for bypass surgery because he had no blockages, thus no stints. His heart muscle was worn out and there wasn't anything that could be done.

J.W. was losing the battle, but as a Christian he would win the war. Each day yielded nothing positive regarding his condition. Our family stuck together and we all rallied around him. We talked to him and he communicated with us by squeezing our hands when his sedation wasn't as intense as other times. My time at home was basically spent making, receiving and returning calls. I will never forget the kindness of others.

It was May 23rd and I sat in the chair by the window in his hospital room. The sun

The Black Widow

beamed on my back which felt good because the room was always cool. I pulled a tattered piece of paper from my purse and wrote a poem about what was and what would never be again, without divine intervention.

In the stillness of the night
Nothing stirring but a breeze
Our breathing was smooth
And all at ease
Our way was clear
For another day
But God saw things in,
yet, a different way
Time slowed down
And then it stood still
Time was no more
It was all in His will
We say goodbye ...
I say goodbye to the
love of my life
He was my husband
And I was his wife
And so the story goes ...

Faye J. Williams

But it was willed to come to an end
Good bye my sweet love
Goodbye my friend

I didn't think I was being pessimistic but more of a realist, a reluctant realist. We were climbing a very slippery slope at best. It was nearing time for the visiting hour to end. A lot of times I didn't respond to the first call. I reasoned that the first call was for everybody else. I didn't gather my purse until the second call. That afternoon when I got home I pulled a few weeds and trimmed some bushes. My plan was also to mow the lawn and set out a few annuals because I wanted the yard to look nice when he came home, even if it was but a dream.

One day, a day or so later, it dawned on me that J.W. may not be able to return to our physical home but to his home **not made with hands**. My emotions broke loose at the seams. There was a part of me that knew or had a strong idea how things were headed. There was a bigger part of me that wanted to

The Black Widow

shove reality off the edge of time. Reality was sending my thoughts in a different direction.

Thursday evening when I arrived home, Jayveun was in the yard tossing his football in the air. I sat in the car a few extra minutes before turning off the ignition. Jayveun, only nine at the time knew how critical his PahPah was. I explained to him that if J.W. did not improve that he won't survive. I was just being real. I don't believe in sugar-coating the truth, no matter how badly it may hurt. I asked Jayveun, point blank, that if J.W. didn't survive would he read the New Testament scripture at his funeral. I love Jayveun to the moon and back, he's strong and courageous, much like his PahPah. He immediately said that he would and then he asked, "*All of it"?* 'No, darling', I said, 'I'll pick out a few passages of scripture for you'. I chose 2 Timothy 4:7-8 ~ *I have fought a good fight, I have finished my course, I have kept the faith; Henceforth there is laid up for me a crown of righteousness, which the Lord, the righteous judge, shall give me at that day: and not to me only, but unto all them also that love his appearing.*

CHAPTER 12

'Hold on, God Will See You Through'

Holding on was all that I had left. I listened to the words of the song, "Hold On", as I drove up 58 Highway headed to Memorial Hospital. Pelts of rain banged on the hood of the car, the thunder roared and the lightning flashed brilliantly in the sky. This was the beginning of the Memorial Day Weekend. J.W. was not showing any signs of improvement and I was in a fog, I heard things and I understood things.

The Black Widow

My body was keeping up yet my heart was behind. At some point my family and I talked about the future and how we were going to move forward regarding J.W.'s care. We all knew how critical he was and we were on the same page. We weren't going to let him continue to be ventilated considering all of his other ailments if his chances of survival were so minimal. We agreed that nothing would take place until after the holiday, not until Tuesday, May 27th.

I pulled on to DeSales Drive and into a covered parking space. The roar of thunder and flashes of lightning reminded me of a storm a few years earlier that bolted me from my sleep. The thunder was incredible. J.W. wrapped his strong arms around me and held me tightly until the storm subsided or I calmed or maybe we stayed that way until morning. That was a bittersweet memory.

Later as I sat in the hospital room the storm began to fade. The gray clouds were replaced by a soft blue canopy and the sun shone as brightly as ever. The hums and beeps continued in the background. J.W. seemed a little restless and his brow was furrowed. I patted his frail arm and held his hand, so did our children. I would watch them watch him. I knew that everyone had their own private thoughts and memories, yet at the core of it all was a wonderful man that we all loved dearly. Shortly the nurse came in and placed some medicine in his IV to help him to relax.

The room grew quiet once again. There was a peck on the door. It was Mr. Whitten, a very nice gentleman who stopped by after leaving his wife's bedside. Mr. Whitten, always very encouraging would often check on J.W. as he and his daughter headed to the elevator. He told me that we were in his prayers. We started as strangers but we ended as friends.

Well it's now Saturday and the holiday is 'on and poppin'. Even though Memorial Day is officially Monday lots of folks have cookouts and get-togethers starting the weekend leading into the holiday. Merchants stock well for the

The Black Widow

holiday and the consumers pull the charcoal, lighter fluid, liquid smoke and the ingredients for their special sauces from the shelves, not to mention the chicken, ribs, ground beef and wieners that will be thrown on grills across the nation. But in the Williams world things were different. Sure we were able to laugh and carry-on about some things but our hearts were torn up. Saturday afternoon, between my hospital visits, Myra brought me a bar-b-cue plate from her sisters' house, where they had gathered earlier for a cook-out. That evening I didn't drive myself back to the hospital for the last visitation, Anne drove me.

Sunday was a particularly busy day. Lots of friends and relatives visited to show their love and concern. Lisa and Donna were there when I arrived for the 8:00 a.m. visit. We stayed until it was nearly time for our church services to begin. When I returned for the afternoon visitation, it was standing room only. Nearly all of the children and grandchildren and lots of friends were on hand. I don't know how much of what J.W. was aware of but he would have been pleased knowing how much people loved him. As soon as Pam and Alesia, his step-daughters, knew how sick he was, they visited immediately. If love, concern and will were all he needed to get well, he would have walked out of the hospital with us that night.

In my mind I revisited the Wednesday before when he was admitted to the hospital and was to be kept overnight for observation. I never, in my wildest imagination, thought that his last time at home was his last time. I really thought that he would have stabilized to some degree, at least to be able to return home and maybe to be able to attend church on Sunday. I continued to pray. I continued to pray for J.W. and to ask for strength, guidance and the ability to accept the Lord's will.

The phone rang early Monday morning, one of J.W.'s cousins called from Detroit for an update. We talked briefly. I poured myself a cup of coffee and let the day ahead settle in my mind. I flipped through the mail that lay on the kitchen table and reread cards that people had mailed us.

"Hold On" played in the distance as I drove to the hospital. The elevator door opened and I stepped onto a well-polished floor and a familiar shift of nurses. Donna and Lisa greeted me as I entered the room. I walked over to J.W., stroked his hand and planted a kiss on his forehead. He had no reaction at all. I told him about the many phone calls and cards that we'd received from well-wishers and how the yard was shaping up. My cell phone buzzed. It was Mama calling to check on us. She wanted so much to help me, to help us but at 95 years old, it took all she had and then some to take care of herself. His sedation was deep. I wondered so desperately what was he thinking, could he think, was he in pain, was he missing me, did he really know how much we loved him. That morning when visitation ended I left the room but sat in the waiting area a few minutes before leaving the hospital. I was feeling confused and I was concerned about Lisa whose birthday was in a few short days. The balance of the visitation times ended with me walking out with family and for brief moments we even talked about stuff totally unrelated to our present situation. A safe diversion was a welcomed diversion even if it was short-lived.

I woke up Tuesday morning from a restless night. I got up and readied myself for the hospital. All kinds of thoughts resonated my mind. My theme song, "Hold On", played as I turned on first one street and then the other until I was by my husband's side. The sun was really showing out. It was a beautiful day for whatever was to come. When I arrived, Donna and Lisa were already there. Chase, Lisa's younger son was in the waiting area. The doctor came in, doctor ...I don't remember his name. Lisa called Veronica, herself a physician, and put her on speaker phone. Veronica was always kept in the loop and she was in communication with J.W.'s doctors. She was also able to explain things to us when we needed additional clarity. We were in agreement not to keep J.W. hooked up any longer. I knew what we said, I knew what I had to do and I wasn't under any duress but when I was presented the documentation making the go-ahead official, it was more than difficult to sign paperwork. It was the most difficult thing that I've ever done. The doctor even told us that J.W. had a fair chance of 'holding his own'. The technicians came in to start the disconnect process. At some point Donna left to take Chase to school. The hums and beeps were silenced. J.W.'s sedation was not nearly as deep as it had been. It was very painful to watch and the tubing in his throat was deep and excruciating to remove. The doctor shook our hands and wished us well. He asked if we had any questions, but questioning time was pretty much over. The doctor, techs and nurse left the room. Lisa was on one side of the bed and I was on the other side. J.W. was restless and his pain level was extreme. J.W. had not been given pain meds to block the insurmountable suffering that he was subjected to. He tried to sit up but we encouraged him to relax, he tried to talk but words didn't come easy. He coughed and it startled me. Lisa noticed that I stepped back. I stepped closer again and asked him if he knew who I was. It was a strain but he managed to muster ..." Myyyyyy... ...wife". I asked him if he knew who she was, talking about Lisa and he said, "Myyyyy ...daughter". His speech was very exaggerated. He called neither of us by name. He was struggling, congested and in extreme pain. I noticed a large wet spot on his top sheet. I lifted the sheet to make sure his catheter was still in place and it was. We called the nurse and told her that he needed to be suctioned and he needed some pain meds. We also told her that he needed clean linen. She came to suction him but the congestion was too deep for her to suction and he was too weak to cough it up. She had a call in the doctor regarding pain meds. Directives should have already been in place. Lisa and I were barely holding on. A second nurse appeared to help

The Black Widow

change the linen. We told them not to bother. We were losing him.

CHAPTER 13

2 Timothy 4:7

All kinds of things were running through my mind. Life was slipping away rapidly. J.W. had a plea in his eyes and a look of fear. His eyes were begging for help and there wasn't anything that we could do. I knew that something was happening, something completely out of our control. I soon came to realize that the congestion in his chest must have been what I had always heard of as the 'death rattle'. He would look at me and then gaze upward. 'Hey, sweetie, I'm here, look this way… …we are here'. He was restless. He would look in my direction, but only briefly. Again he gazed upward. We held his hands and told him to relax. We told him how much we loved him. He would look at us and then upward again. He applied pressure to my hand. It didn't hurt but it was firm. The pain meds never came. After a short while he calmed down and the panic in his eyes was gone. He relaxed and closed his eyes, a pinkish white foamy substance spilled from his mouth and he was gone. My husband, my precious husband, our children's father, my soulmate was gone.

    I screamed, 'he's gone, he's gone' and buried my face on his arm. Lisa and I cried and cried. Donna returned either just before or just after it was over. His hands were soft and smooth and all the pain was gone from his face.

    The nurse checked his vitals. The doctor and the nurse extended their condolences. We were all changed instantly, immediately on the spot. We stabbed numbers on our cell phones and gathered our family together. Lisa and

Jade dialed Ashley's number repeatedly without a response. She was at work but in an exercise class with her manager. Her phone was in her locker. When she got to her phone, she had been tagged on a Facebook post, **Rest in Peace Uncle J.W.** Not the way to find out that your father has just died. Oh, my Lord, how horrible.

In the twinkling of an eye
In the swift of a moment
My life changed forever
Though quiet was the room
No rhythm to detect
No wind in the pipes, the drumsticks at rest
The soul was on the brink of its marvelous return
The angels stood by as he finished his race
They took what mattered to a better place
No crackling of the body
As the spirit broke free
I held his hand and cried relentlessly
In the twinkling of an eye
I was married, then I was not

The Black Widow

*My familiar world was changed immediately
on the spot
I now must walk this lonely road
My memories will help me through
"One day at a time", I'm often told
"Just do the best that you can do"
I cry myself to sleep some nights
And others I can't remember
But that's okay so they say
It's all a part of healing
I brace myself when dark reaches dawn
And life awakens beneath the sky
Another day has broken
Another day without the familiar
Another day has broken
But hope is just over yonder
Over the hill are hope and healing
Just over the hill is hope*
June 4, 2014

CHAPTER 14

Now What?

Mama has always said that you can't begin the journey to healing or begin to get over a death until after the burial. One thing that she never said was how long after the loss will the healing start. And she didn't mean, 'get over', she meant 'adjust'. Some things you never get over.

First of all, know this: Grief is very relative and personal. Every loss is different. Even if you lose the same familial component in your life that someone else has in theirs' that doesn't equate to identical grieving. Nothing does.

Grief is an emotion, grieving is a perpetuation of that emotion. Grieving does not have an expiration date. But like everything else in life we have to learn to put grief in perspective. It's not easy but it is doable. In the beginning you don't see that as a possibility but through patience and Christ all things are possible.

Please understand, grief is not a state that you get over. It is a reality, a presence that you learn to manage. The person that you are grieving will always be gone and that is a fact that will never change. The change will be on our end, on the survivor's end. We have to change how we think, how we live, how we breathe and even how we shop. That may sound simple, maybe even silly but when it's a husband/wife team and half of the whole is no longer present the balance of that team must then learn how to grocery shop and cook for one. That's a learned process. Take for instance, that head of cabbage that the two of

Faye J. Williams

you used to dine off of for a couple of meals each. That wasn't so bad but just try eating that cabbage for four meals and there's still some left over.

It's a grappling experience going to the grocery store for the first few times as a new widow. I remember going up and down a few isles at Walmart, a couple of weeks after my husband died, and spotting items that I used to purchase solely for him ...pork & beans, honey buns and Vienna sausage, just to name a few items. It brought tears to my eyes. I was a wreck and I felt like bolting from the store and dashing home. But that would not have solved anything. I still had to grocery shop. That was simply one of many instances that proved to me that I couldn't run away from my feelings, that I had to face the hand that I'd been dealt.

No one can prepare you to lose your husband. I know lots of women who are widows but not one of them could make my pain go away. A hug, a pat, a nod of understanding, an assurance that not every day would be black, all those things were good but my pain still pulsated violently.

In the beginning, everything is grappling. From the day, the moment my husband died, everything from that moment on became a 'first'. In almost 30 years I had not seen a sunrise or a sunset without my husband. That doesn't mean that he was literally by my side at every sun up and sun down but he was somewhere close by.

Not every day, immediately following the death and burial, will you cry your eyes out. But, just because you seem to have some tolerable days early in the grieving process, don't think that you have a handle on it. What you actually have is a false positive. I had to learn that, among so many things, the hard way. One day I would feel in charge. I felt like I was handling my loss and making progress in the right direction. That might last for a week or so and then another day my world was closing in on me and I was overwhelmed with grief and confusion. Not confusion in the sense that chaos was brewing, but confusion in that my hands were doing this, my mind was thinking that, I couldn't focus and the tears would start to flow all over again. I just sobbed, the shoulder shaking kind of sobbing.

A couple of months after my husband died, I was at the same funeral home visiting with a family that had just embarked on this dreadful journey. While there a friend approached me, a little surprised that I was there in light of my recent loss. She asked me how I was doing and I told her okay, sometimes, as long as no one asked me any hard questions. She sort of narrowed her eyes and repeated, *Hard questions?* I told her that a hard question could be something like someone looking me dead in the eye, and asking me how was I *really* doing or something as simple as, *what time is it?* It could so happen to be the time that my husband died. So basically to sum it up on some days any and everything can be difficult. Actually several people were surprised to see me there. Not being there wasn't going to make my pain any less or being there wasn't going to make it greater. That was one of the early days that I had control.

Everyone has heard the old adage that you can't judge a book by its cover. How true that is. Just because the apple is shining on the outside doesn't mean that it's not crumbling on the inside. I've often felt like that apple. People would remark that I seemed to be doing well. I continued my normal exterior fix-ups, you know, hair, nails, clothing, make-up, but on the inside I was a wreck. That also reminds me of a skillet of cornbread that I made once. It was so pretty and brown on the outside and it smelled so good. But when I sliced into it, it was a whole different undone, story.

Grief is a peculiar thing and it's perplexing but it is manageable. Manageable on your terms and your time frame.

CHAPTER 15

Understanding and Acceptance

With grief comes understanding and acceptance. As a Christian I understand that God giveth and God taketh away. However, being equipped with that knowledge does not eradicate the profound heartache that engulfs the bereavement arena. Oh, yes, I know that there is a God, a Sovereign being but I was still in pain.

I do not say understanding and acceptance casually because in the full scheme of things

The Black Widow

whether we understand it or not or whether we accept it or not there is no negotiating. A much higher power has made a decision. God never makes a bad decision or a mistake. No matter how we may sometimes feel.

We have many Biblical examples of grief and how certain subjects managed. Take David, for instance. He said in Psalm 30:5 ~ *For His anger is but for a moment. His favor is for life. Weeping may endure for a night. But joy comes in the morning.* In essence, our pain will come and our pain will go. And the process will be repeated, time and again. Eventually the pain will come with less intensity.

Solomon recognized the profoundness of grief in, seasonal terms, in Ecclesiastes 3. Particularly in verse 4: *A time to weep and a time to laugh; a time to mourn and a time to dance.* In reading these scriptures, you will notice that David, a man after God's own heart and Solomon, a man known for his wisdom, didn't give a time-frame for grieving. So why should we?

During the course of writing this book, there were a couple of times that I simply had to hit 'save' and shut the computer down. You see, from the beginning I knew how my story would end, I just didn't realize that reliving the past would be so difficult. As the first anniversary of J.W.'s death neared, I became increasingly emotional. I managed the anniversary fairly well but the following day as I made some entries in my book I became overwhelmed with grief. I was home alone weeping uncontrollably when my phone rang. I looked at the display on the phone. It was my dear friend Myra calling to check on me. I was crying so hard that I couldn't even say hello. Not one time did she tell me not to cry, she told me to cry it out. She stayed on the phone with me until I caught my breath and she knew that I would be okay. I cried until I had no more tears. It was a perfect cleansing for that moment.

CHAPTER 16

The Anatomy of Grief

I have heard this and I've verified it through research that the grieving process has steps. Every article that I've read claimed that there are five to seven steps and each article identified anger as part of that process. And, in my opinion, a feeling of being inadequate, being pushed into something that you've neither asked for nor wanted ought to be some place at the top of the steps. Like Lisa, who is also a widow, said to me one day, '*I didn't ask for this. This is not what I signed on for. I don't want to be in this club*'. Lisa, by the way, has been and continues to be an invaluable source of help, strength and encouragement to me. A real right arm, so to speak.

I guess that being angry really depends on the circumstance, how and why your loved one died. Had my husband been gunned down, or killed by an intoxicated driver or some other foolish mishap I would likely feel differently. My heart is lonely and I ache for him but I'm not and I never have been '*mad at God', the Creator of every good and perfect gift.*

Also in grieving, that particular person that you're mourning means many different things to different people. But when you lose your spouse, you lose someone who pretty much knows you inside out. When J.W. transitioned he left behind a host of loved ones and friends, who they lost and who I lost was not on the same level.

Some people have said to me that they know **exactly** how I feel because they lost their mother or father or sibling or best friend or ...and it goes on and on. In reality they don't know **exactly** how I feel. No one does.

Faye J. Williams

What they have done is put grief in a basket and generalized it. And you can't do that. Please believe me, I am not trying to minimize anyone's grief or well- intentions. People are very kind and they simply want you to know during your time of grief and sorrow that you're not alone, that they, too, have experienced grief on some level. I get it! So very often people want to console you but they don't know how. Sometimes a gentle pat or a hug speaks volumes.

I have dear loved ones and friends who have lost a spouse. They come closer to understanding my feelings than anyone else. And even with that they don't know **exactly** how I feel, they know how they felt. Sometimes it seems to me that people feel that they just have to say something. Wrong. One friend sent me a text one day offering condolences. She also said to let her know if I needed anything and she ended the text by saying that if I just needed someone to sit with me, just let her know. To me that was profound. Because by saying, ***just sit with***

The Black Widow

me, that meant that we didn't have to talk, that meant that I could rest or do nothing, that meant that I didn't have to try to be a hostess, that meant that I just didn't have to be alone. Thank you, Sandra Gail Odom.

CHAPTER 17

Pause Before You Post

We live in a time like no other. We have social media, we have electronic communications, we have instant messaging, we have cell phones, you name it we have it. We can transmit information faster than a microwave oven can soften an Idaho potato. But with all that stuff we have going on, nothing takes the place of common courtesy and communication etiquette.

When death happens please stifle the urge to put condolences, your RIP's and RIH's on Facebook immediately. Truly I

The Black Widow

know that you want to get your concern and sympathy out there promptly but try to hold off doing so until you're sure that immediate family members know. Sometimes repeated attempts, such as the case when Lisa and Jade were trying to reach Ashley, have been made to reach certain people that are either away from their phone or otherwise out of pocket but they don't need to be tagged on a Facebook post that their mother, father, sister or brother or… ...has died. That is ***not*** a good way to find out. I am thankful that Ashley wasn't alone when she read the post.

    At the end of the day or even the next day is soon enough for a post. Granted, nowadays, the social media community is like a family in some instances, however, all I'm saying is think before you post. We could all use a little social media etiquette. A card in the mail is still a stylish way to communicate. Once those that should know are aware, feel free to acknowledge the loss of an individual and express concern and sympathy to those in bereavement. Social media and electronic devices are invaluable means of instant communication.

Everybody, in my opinion, that is going through the process of grieving needs to find ways to channel their feelings. One of my outlets is through the written word. Grieving is hard by any stretch of the imagination, and nobody can tell you how to do it. There are some things that you do that you just simply have to cry and do it. For instance, the first time that I changed the linen on our bed after J.W. died. That was very hard because he had lain on those sheets. His deoxyribonucleic acid (DNA) was there; his smell was there but the reality is that I had to do laundry no matter what. I felt like I was washing him away. That's all a part of the de-webbing.

One thing that I figured out early on is that loved ones and friends are absolutely indispensable. As your friends and family rally around you with offers to help, let them help. They carry you on and urge you forward. Sometimes when people asked me what I needed or wanted them to do I couldn't think of anything. Friends often remind you to eat and sometimes certain ones will say something like, '**here, eat this'.**

    Always bear in mind that not everybody is comfortable with everything. This goes for friends and family. It is important that people are honest with you and that you allow people to be honest. I remember the day that J.W. died and we were finally leaving the hospital, Donna told me that she'd help in every way that she could but that there were some things she couldn't do. And so I said to her what is it that you can't do and she said that she couldn't do the funeral home stuff…like picking out caskets and stuff. No problem. Not everybody can do everything. When there are things that you are simply not comfortable with, speak up, that's very important. But what Donna did do was enormous. I think that it's important not to let your grief become an imposition on anyone. Just remember that you aren't the only one grieving.

Also as we were leaving the hospital I made the statement that I was going home alone. I needed to think. I thought that I needed to be alone. As I was driving home, my theme song playing softly in the background, some lady from a tissue bank called me. I told her that I presently was in no condition to talk to her. She apologized, offered her condolences and asked if she could call later. I told her that she could. I really needed to concentrate on driving. I wasn't crying at that moment, and I was trying to stay calm. I was numb. Death sparks some unusual feelings. I knew that J.W. was dead but even while driving home, I felt an urge to go back to the hospital to be with him. Strange, huh?

Finally, at home, I unlocked the door and walked into the house, the first time as a widow. The first time that our home wasn't our home. But I did announce that I was going home alone. I had only been home a short while when I got a text from my friend of over fifty years. Without looking outside,

The Black Widow

I answered the text and told Sharron that I had opted to come home alone, just to be by myself for a while. I didn't know that she was in the driveway at the time. She texted me right back and said that she was pulling out of my driveway and that she would call me later. I immediately read her response and told her not to go. I'm so glad she stayed. I only thought that I wanted to be alone. Sharron, also a widow, guided me through the call when the tissue bank lady called back.

CHAPTER 18

The Strength of Others

When I started writing this book, I wanted it to be not only for those in bereavement but also for those offering condolences and assistance. Sort of a do's and don'ts. Everybody will face grief at some point. Hopefully this book will serve as a source of solace for those going through the process. For those who haven't faced bereavement perhaps this book will contain something that can be laid in store and when the time comes excerpts can be used to help in that troublesome time.

The Black Widow

When you are going through this process, there are no 'Gone with The Wind' moments ...*after all, tomorrow is another day*. Yes, tomorrow is another day but some things have to be handled now. Don't plan to make any decisions alone. This is also not the time for family feuding, if you have a feuding family. Whether you have pre-arranged the service or if you are starting from scratch you need loving, patient and coherent people with you throughout the process.

Lisa was my right-hand girl. My sister, brother-in-law and Ashley were also with me but Lisa was the voice of experience. And it wasn't always what they said but having them there meant everything. They were my function when I couldn't function. They never pushed me or rushed me and the funeral director, Anita Taylor, is also a friend and so with those key people the outcome was pretty seamless. I appreciated and accepted advice because I needed it. Sometimes throughout the process I felt like a zombie. I remember being stuck on choosing a casket. I favored

Faye J. Williams

one, my sister favored another. I don't remember if Lisa and Ashley expressed an opinion one way or the other. Finally, James picked out one to break the ice. It was a big white ugly thing ...totally out of the question. We sort of laughed, made a decision and moved on. Another hold up for me was the use of the word, **devoted**, in the obituary to describe my role. In reading so many obituaries I just thought that the word **devoted** was worn out and needed a break. Even though it was very accurate and descriptive. Lisa, Anne and Ashley threw out many other words but in the final analysis **devoted** was the best word to use. There was also a question of what picture to use for the program. I had the idea to use a picture that was taken of J.W. and me on his 75th birthday. Evidently that wasn't a good idea. My family said that we should use a different picture for an obvious reason, I wasn't deceased. Anita finally spoke up and said, "Faye, no!" Of course, they were right. We completed what had to be done at the funeral home at that time, then we had the cemetery to contend with. By this time, I was nearly completely wiped out. But my job wasn't complete.

My mind started wandering and I felt anxious. I felt like I needed to be home or at the hospital or just someplace else. In reality I was where I needed to be. I was where I had to be. No one was anyplace awaiting my return. My husband was gone. We went to the cemetery and took care of the paperwork and planning there. I wasn't aware that the cemetery had so many sections and each section had a name. I can remember the director pointing in this direction and that direction calling each section by name. This was a hard process but I wasn't alone. I wasn't the only one hurting and grieving. I never took the attitude that I'm the grieving widow and everything was about me. Everything was about each of us. We were family before, we were family during and we would always be family. I never wanted to create friction with anyone. I have heard it said more than once, how people misbehave

Faye J. Williams

and really act up sometimes when there's been a death but it's so unnecessary. Sometimes people even fight and for what, I ask. This is the time to pull together, to work together.

    A couple of days later I'm home alone, feeling a little weary and kind of on edge. The only sound in the house is the pendulum of my grandfather clock gliding north and south, my heartbeat and my soft sobs. I am missing my mate. I want to go to him and be with him but those days are over, I remind myself. My mind reels. I go upstairs and climb into bed. Rest won't come. Sleep won't come. I pray and cry. '**Lord, please take this pain away or just give me the strength to bear it'.** Eventually the night came to a close and it was the next day. I thought about a poem that I had written for a friend, just over a year earlier, when she started her journey on this lonesome road.

The Black Widow

The Day After

The sun rose again the next day
I always knew that it would
Our time together had come to an end
Like the sun, I rose and started to mend
I sat alone quietly in a chair
Not even wanting to comb my hair
I sipped my first cup of coffee
No longer as your wife
The pain in my heart
Was as a piercing with a knife
I told myself, 'Don't go there, girl. Get up and move on'
But the thought of that progression was a chill to the bone
The sun rose again the next day
I always knew that it would
I rolled out of bed
And did the best I could
I laughed out loud when I stumbled over your shoe
I used to get so mad ...so angry at you
I fried a strip of bacon
The aroma wafted through the air

*I poured a cup of coffee
And eased into your chair
One day at a time is all that I can do
But God's amazing grace will always see me through*
Written for my friend, Sibley P. Hines, January 23, 2013

When we met at the funeral home the morning of the wake for the family viewing, J.W.'s hands were covered and Veronica wanted his hands uncovered. He looked beautiful and pain-free. He did have nice hands so making sure that his hands were uncovered was no problem. Lisa mentioned to me either that morning or sometime the day before that if I wanted to we could have friends and family gather at Donna's house after the wake. That way, she said, when you get tired and want to rest you can go home and do so, without feeling like you're abandoning guests. I said earlier that Lisa guided me through a lot of the processes and she did. I also said that

The Black Widow

Donna mentioned that she couldn't do the funeral home stuff but what she did was absolutely enormous. I mean it. She opened up her home and people poured in and when I left to go home there were still lots of people there. That was a big deal and I truly appreciated it. Working together is key. There is absolutely nothing like love, family and friendships.

CHAPTER 19

Embracing a New Normal

Now that the funeral service is over there are still tasks to be completed. The acknowledgments and the tough task of restoring order to your home. By now everyone has gone back to their respective routines and it was up to me to try to put my life back together and nurture a 'new normal'. Everyone knows the saying, 'life goes on'. And it does. I couldn't stop going to church, or grocery shopping or working or any of the other things that I did

The Black Widow

before I became a widow. J.W. died in May so I still had months of yard work to do. I had taken on the responsibility of managing the yard work a few years earlier. By any measure of the stick, yard work is hard work. The first time I mowed the lawn after J.W.'s death was the hardest of all. Although he could no longer do the work, he always critiqued my work, he watched out for me and he would encourage me to come inside and take a break and refresh myself. Just knowing he was there made a big difference. Sometimes if it wasn't too hot he'd sit outside for a while. Even though I was tremendously familiar with my outside work, it just wasn't the same. Nothing was the same. Sometimes as I pushed the mower, I also pushed back tears.

    I cried a lot and I thought of him constantly. I tried to go back to work a couple of days following the funeral but that didn't work for me, I wasn't ready yet and I was fortunate to be able to take a little more time off. But I still had to do something constructive.

One friend suggested grief counseling, so I did go for one visit and I should have gone maybe a few more times but my insurance didn't cover this particular counselor with whom I connected. Once I found out that she was out of network I didn't have the resolve to start over. So my one visit to a grief counselor was my only visit.

A few days following the funeral my friends, Kellye, Mary, and Sarah took me to dinner. We went to Famous Dave's. It was nice. My friends were still carrying me. Kellye asked me if I felt like driving or if I wanted someone to pick me up. I was fine to drive. I was determined to take advantage of my good days because as sure as my name is Faye I knew that there would be an avalanche of dark days ahead. We talked about J.W. They let me go on and on. We all attend church together, so they had their own memories. I needed that time. I even laughed.

Now what? I know that God is there, and I have faith that He will continue to bless me. I also know that faith without works is dead. What that means to me is that I have some work to do. I will continue to have lots of ups and downs. I still have a rocky road ahead of me that I must navigate. Actually rocky is an understatement ...boulders are more like it.

It is important, as we navigate this process, not to shut people out and work at clearing some things away, strictly at your own pace. My husband was on oxygen, and he had a very long tube. When I came home from the hospital, the day he died, one of the first things that I did was to disconnect the tube from the machine and toss it in the garbage. Granted, there was no urgency, but I didn't need to look at the tube knowing that he would never be at the other end of it.

Sharron, my friend, whose husband died a few years earlier, often said to me, **"you will just have to ride it out."**

I couldn't just sit back and feel sorry for myself. God has His reasons and motives, and I still had to work hard to develop some traction so that my steps forward wouldn't be in vain. Traction doesn't come over night.

It's important to pay attention to what you are doing and thinking. There were days that I found myself sitting in the quiet of my home, no TV, no noise, no nothing. I stayed in bed far too long and occasionally dark thoughts skipped through my mind. I actually made no attempts to contact people, but I didn't shy away from phone calls. I wasn't angry, I wasn't in a, 'why me, Lord?' mode, I think that I was numb and tired. Numb, tired and missing my husband. I would read my Bible some days and study my Bible some days. I was still able to thank God for being merciful. My husband was sick, and he had suffered and the Great I Am gave him rest. In all things, thank God. I figured that it was better to have loved and lost than to never have loved at all.

When death knocks you to your knees, and it will, you have to make a conscious effort to breathe, to move and to not be imprisoned by it.

The Black Widow

Sometimes, if you aren't careful, you can find yourself sinking. Depression is a dangerous thing. I was not in a good place. But thankfully I didn't continue along that path. I didn't do much but I, at least, made myself get up and brush my teeth. That was something. I knew that I couldn't allow myself to succumb to my grief. After all, I did have family that was concerned about me, and I was concerned about them also. I hired a friend to video the funeral for me. The first time that I watched it, I saw some things that I hadn't seen before. The second time that I watched it, it was at my mothers' house. She was unable to attend the service due to her own afflictions. I didn't cry either time. I was thankful for the show of love and concern.

Don't be afraid to tell people how you feel when they ask. They don't expect you to rehearse everything from day one. And reasonable people know that your feelings today are subject to change tomorrow. And know that it's okay. Your healing is based on you and your timetable, not anyone else's. But it's also important not to fight healing.

CHAPTER 20

A New Season

Somehow I managed to make it through the balance of 2014, what would have been his birthday, the holidays and what would have been our anniversary. My struggles aren't as great as they were, and I'm adjusting to being alone. Missing my husband is something that I will always do. I miss our drive to church on Sunday mornings and sitting next to him during service. When we sing certain songs in church, I still tear up, especially when we sing, "Hard Fighting Soldier."

The Black Widow

I recently attended a Prayer Breakfast, and I asked the ladies that were present to please pray for my family and me as we were nearing 10 months since my husband's death. This Prayer Breakfast was hosted by the Shepherd Church of Christ where I attend. There were lots of women there, and a lot of them are widows. One lady, in particular, talked with me, and she encouraged me using words that my mother had used to encourage her when her husband died almost 9 years earlier.

Even though fall and winter have passed, those seasons brought with them a new sense of missing my husband. For instance, in the fall, he would gather wood for the wood burner. I learned to appreciate the smell of wood. When he'd gotten to the point that it was no longer safe for him to manage the wood burner, I did it. I paid attention to his instructions and learned quickly. The winter was simply more of the same. With the dark nights coming quickly and I was still scrambling with my new normal, I worked almost feverishly to get things done before it was black outside. As a widow, living alone, you have to be careful of your environment. When I got home from work, I set my purse down and immediately went outside to gather wood for the wood burner, or if the next day was garbage pick-up, I worked quickly to put out my garbage and my neighbor's garbage. I developed a routine and stuck with it.

CHAPTER 21

Healing Not Healed

Difficult days are still a part of my healing. But I am healing. I haven't dreamed about my husband, and yet I want to. I want to dream about him as a healthy man. I want to touch him and hold him and talk with him. My husband is still a part of who I am. About a month after his death I took his wedding band to a jeweler and had it sized to fit my finger. Each morning, as I dress, I slip his wedding band on my finger. Not expecting the ring to give him back to me but I like touching something that he touched every day.

It's imperative that we don't deny ourselves the process of healing. Each person heals in a different way, but if a year has passed and there has been no progress on your part, something is wrong with that picture. The old adage, 'time brings about a change' and it does or it certainly should.

One thing that we must do is learn to be comfortable with ourselves. We have to learn to take care of ourselves. I'm not speaking about the widows that have health issues or mental decline or those that are elderly and cannot care for themselves. But for those that can, we must.

I remember one Sunday at church, I was really having a hard time. That particular Sunday, only a few weeks after my husband's death, I was really struggling with my loss and my emotions were out of control. One daughter had been planning for a few months to leave the nest and another daughter was planning to move back out, leaving me home alone. My Minister asked me if my daughters would be willing to stay with me a little longer, delaying their plans, just until I was better. I didn't want that. I would not have even asked that of them. I wasn't afraid to be alone; I was just overcome with grief. He thought that being alone was also a part of what I was feeling, but it wasn't. I was willing to make adjustments because, basically, I had no choice but I wasn't willing to impose on anyone's plans for my purpose.

Having them delay their plans was not the answer. The answer was accepting, embracing and learning to let go. Accepting what had happened, embracing what remained, and learning to let go of what was gone. Had I asked them to stay, they would have, but that would not have accomplished anything for them or me.

When J.W. and I married, I moved from my parents' home to his home. I had never lived on my own. I was venturing into a whole new phase of my life. One that I hadn't anticipated. What I had to realize was

The Black Widow

that I was housekeeping on a whole different level. I had to make my own decisions, and I was responsible for myself.

I recently had dinner with four girlfriends. Three are married, and the fourth friend was widowed two months after I was. She had been married for 52 years. What a long time. Anyway, when I first talked to her after her husband's death, she was planning to do some work on her house and put it on the market. And she had some other thoughts that she shared. Some of what she said to me, I heard and some I didn't because I was stuck on the house part. And, at the time, she was spending nights away from home. She had diligently started looking at other real estate with the assistance of a realtor. During dinner, I asked her what did she ever decide to do about the house. She announced that she was staying put. I was happy to hear that. She went on to say that she's a '*big girl,*' that during her time of looking around, she discovered, real estate less than what she had was more expensive. She also mentioned that the repairs that she needed to have done had been taken care of, and the perimeter of her house had been cleared. All she really had to do was pray earnestly about it and wait on the Lord. *Ain't God good? He's a mighty good God!* I just love Isaiah 40:31 ~ *But they that wait upon the Lord shall renew their strength; they shall mount up with wings as eagles; they shall run, and not be weary, and they shall walk and not faint.*

Another dear friend that was widowed shortly after I was made a significant change in her housing. She actually powered down from a large home to a more manageable condominium. And it's fine to do that, just make sure that your decisions are properly driven. When all is said and done, you still want to feel confident that you did the right thing.

The difference between the two friends is that one considered an action that was fear driven and the other was desire driven. Where there is fear, and we act upon that fear, there will likely be regret down the line.

CHAPTER 22

It's Time to Fly

There are so many memories tucked away in my mind, and I would be selfish if I didn't share them. I've mentioned that when friends and family offer their assistance, those weakened by circumstance have a responsibility to accept. No matter how we may think, at times, we really can't do it all.

And I believe that God places people in our path to help us get over the humps in our lives.

The Black Widow

Countless people reached out to me during my husband's illness and death. Mary and Dixie were two such people.

Dixie would call me nearly every day at different times of the day and Mary would call me every morning as she drove to work and sometimes after she arrived at work. They were both very steadfast. And I was always happy to hear their voices. About a week or so after J.W. died, I noticed that the calls became less frequent. As the days continued to pass, the calls tapered even more and then they stopped. I don't even know that one knew that the other was calling but as time marched on I deciphered their behavior as mother birds. They carried me, and nurtured me, and they slowly saw me gaining strength. And as they did, they started backing away. Now, they weren't too far away because I'd see them weekly at church. They helped me to heal. I will always love them.

This is all a part of healing. That's why it's so important not to shut people out. People, by nature, have healing powers and when we are vulnerable we need that.

These are the kinds of lessons that we must learn so that when it's our time to help someone over the humps of life, we will know what to do. And it's not always about the outward show of affection, love, and concern, it's also about the talks with God that we have on behalf of ourselves and others. Prayer is a powerful tool!

I'm a firm believer in *'thus saith the Lord'*. And I also believe that every scripture is important. With that said, it surely comes as no surprise that I'm a firm believer in not letting the sun set on my wrath. Ephesians 4:26 ~ *Be ye angry and sin not. Let not the sun go down upon your wrath*. Always settle your differences. If you can't resolve your differences before you go to bed at least agree to drop it, if you can, until an agreed upon, more convenient time. You have to learn to pick your 'fights.' Not everything is worth a battle. And I'm not saying that I never went to bed angry or that every day in my marriage

The Black Widow

was Sunday but I am so thankful to God that the issues we had were completely put to rest about 4 or 5 months before his death.

I believe that my healing process would have been more difficult, and challenging had we *left water simmering in the pot.*

CHAPTER 23

Know Your Worth

We have to discover the worthiness in everything that we do. You may even ask yourself, 'what's in it for me'? Whatever you do with a glad heart, that's for the benefit of someone else, there's something there for you.

What made our marriage work was our love and commitment to one another. Our solidarity was genuine and blessed. Now it's all up to me to continue on, strengthened by what we had and hoped for.

The Black Widow

One thing that I often think about is that God took my husband, but He left me here. I must be here for a purpose. My purpose is not to wallow in what I lost but to embrace what I have. Among the many things that I have are some of the most loving, kind and endearing family and friends in the world.

The grieving continues long after the burial. Certain smells and sounds trigger memories, and that's okay. Most days are good. I am managing my new normal. My thoughts are often with J.W., In the beginning, I thought about my husband all day every day. Now I think about him every day just not all day of every day. That doesn't mean that I love him any less, that just means that I'm healing.

My mind keeps reeling
With that lonesome feeling
Wishing you back with me
But I know
Oh, I know that's an impossibility

Faye J. Williams

I can't help feeling like I do
I can't help missing you
Tho' tomorrow is a brand new day
I'll end it the very same way
Missing you, missing you,
missing you
January 11, 2015 ~ 11:24p.m.

My worth is to be a beacon of hope for someone else. To help others as I've been helped. How we grieve is personal. But I do know that life is fragile and short at best. I also know that the God I serve is a relationship God, and He never intended for any of us to be alone. Even when the chilling hand of death grabs our loved one, we're not alone because Jesus tells us in John 14:18 that He would not leave us comfortless. When we find ourselves burdened with grief, it helps when we can pick our situation apart, and that won't happen right away. It helps when we can look at the big picture. The big picture being that it isn't so much about the person being gone but that the person was here. That we were privileged to have known and loved that individual. How much richer our lives were made.

King Solomon said it best in Ecclesiastes when he pronounced that there's a season for everything. And there is. My season with my husband came and went, but it was worth it. There's that ***worth*** again.

When I'm feeling down and lonely, I don't generally involve anyone else in that because they may be having a terrific day and besides, after a bit, my loneliness will fade, and my worthiness will take over. And not only that, Jesus is only a prayer away.

When I see couples out and about I want to go to the woman and tell her to hold his hand a little tighter, embrace a bit longer because sometimes it's over way too soon.

Grief is a dark place, like a cave, and we have to crawl out of it. When we love someone, and that person is plucked away, our options are few. We can either stop and stand still and allow our grief to consume us, or we can stop and stand still as we slowly and painstakingly figure out our moving forward and create a new normal. Death happens, and it is not a respecter of persons. I have said this before, but it is worthy of repeating ~ It's not as much about our loved one being gone as it is that our loved one was here. That we had time with that person.

I had a lifetime with my husband and for that gift, I will always be grateful!

Another thing that I've learned, over time, is that anger isn't always anger. Sometimes it's fear. There were times when J.W. did things that really ticked me off. In retrospect I wasn't always angry, at times I was scared.

Epilogue

Marriage is like boarding the interstate. Two lanes merge into one and then you continue in one direction. Ahead of you are bumps, congestion, a little road rage, people cutting you off, clear driving and then 'bam' out of nowhere comes the unexpected.

Marriage is much like that…with all the verities and intricacies of traffic. It's no longer about the individuals as individuals but as an individual unit.

We take off on a journey as life partners. We are in love, and that love deepens with time. It's understood, from the beginning, that even under the best of circumstances, that sometimes individuals will butt heads. But what we're not prepared for are the things and situations that really set us off course.

We say, "I do" to our vow to nurture and care for one another in sickness and in health, for richer and for poorer. It's easy to say so because we're in love. Sometimes, when certain situations manifest, we then and only then actually realize that love is more than a romantic emotion. It brings the trueness to the phrase, 'love is what it does'.

As we continue down that road of matrimony, our hearts still flutter when we see our component, when we smell our component and when that person is not himself or herself we pick up on that. We can see in one another's eyes if there's a problem, we can tell by the way he touches or she touches ...love and patience and time teach us these things.

Marriage is a beautiful institution, instituted by God and our mate should be the most important person in our physical lives. And if we're blessed to spend decade upon decade upon decade upon decade with that person, how wonderful is that? Our mate is our strength, our mate is the calm after the storm, our mate is our encouragement.

At the onset of marriage, we are in the spring of our lives, no matter how old we are when we embark on the journey. During our marriage, the seasons change many times.

Faye J. Williams

One day we will look at our image in the mirror, and we won't see the person that we used to see. No, we will see a face with folds, and creases, a hairline punctuated with silver and eyes that have dimmed with time. We are now in the fall of our lives. We were conquerors, now we are as a ballad, a sweet, simmering time when our love has mellowed completely into the trenches of our soul.

Invariably a marriage will come to an end. And when it does we must face the challenges that lie ahead. We, sometimes, have to say 'goodbye' to that very soul that we walked with and talked with and loved so deeply. Sometimes we reach the end of the road. No more merging the lanes. But a life spent with someone that you've loved, someone that you've been privileged to grow with and merge with, with all of its complexities and verities, is a life worth living over and over again, season after season.

Written for Mary and Dewery Davenport, November 18, 2014, to commemorate their 40th Wedding Anniversary

Love, Faye

Made in the USA
Columbia, SC
10 March 2023